Sex Check Your Sex Life
100 Checks Sex, Dates, Intimacy

JL Silver

Each person gets their own set:

Man: 50 Checks

Woman: 50 Checks

To Spice Up Sex Life

Copyright © 2015 JL Silver

All rights reserved.

ISBN: 10: 1522896732
ISBN-13: 978-1522896739

First Set of 50 Checks

Tear Here Across This Line

DATE: _____

Sex Check 002

PAY TO THE
ORDER OF: _____

GOING OUT: One Night Of Fun Followed By Sensual Passionate Love

- ☐ Dancing
- ☐ Drinking
- ☐ Movies
- ☐ Bowling
- ☐ Concert
- ☐ Other _____ *Write In Your Own*

- ☐ Blowjob
- ☐ Eating Out
- ☐ Missionary
- ☐ Doggystyle
- ☐ On top
- ☐ Other _____ *Write In Your Own*

- ☐ Car
- ☐ Bed
- ☐ Kitchen
- ☐ Hotel
- ☐ Outside
- ☐ Other _____ *Write In Your Own*

- ☐ Quickie
- ☐ 1 Hour
- ☐ Tantric
- ☐ BDSM Play
- ☐ Toys
- ☐ All Night Long

WHEN: ☐ Monday ☐ Tuesday ☐ Wednesday ☐ Thursday ☐ Friday ☐ Saturday ☐ Sunday

To Be Paid By _____   Signed _____

Back Side Of Check

Tear Here Across This Line

DATE: _____

SEX CHECK DD3

PAY TO THE
ORDER OF: _____

GOING OUT: One Night Of Fun Followed By Sensual Passionate Love

- ☐ Dancing
- ☐ Drinking
- ☐ Movies
- ☐ Bowling
- ☐ Concert
- ☐ Other _____ Write In Your Own

- ☐ Blowjob
- ☐ Eating Out
- ☐ Missionary
- ☐ Doggystyle
- ☐ On top
- ☐ Other _____ Write In Your Own

- ☐ Car
- ☐ Bed
- ☐ Kitchen
- ☐ Hotel
- ☐ Outside
- ☐ Other _____ Write In Your Own

- ☐ Quickie
- ☐ 1 Hour
- ☐ Tantric
- ☐ BDSM Play
- ☐ Toys
- ☐ All Night Long

WHEN: ☐ Monday ☐ Tuesday ☐ Wednesday ☐ Thursday ☐ Friday ☐ Saturday ☐ Sunday

To Be Paid By _____   Signed _____

Back Side Of Check

Tear Here Across This Line

DATE: _____

SEX CHECK 004

PAY TO THE
ORDER OF: _____

GOING OUT: One Night Of Fun Followed By Sensual Passionate Love

- ☐ Dancing
- ☐ Drinking
- ☐ Movies
- ☐ Bowling
- ☐ Concert
- ☐ Other _____ Write In Your Own

- ☐ Blowjob
- ☐ Eating Out
- ☐ Missionary
- ☐ Doggystyle
- ☐ On top
- ☐ Other _____ Write In Your Own

- ☐ Car
- ☐ Bed
- ☐ Kitchen
- ☐ Hotel
- ☐ Outside
- ☐ Other _____ Write In Your Own

- ☐ Quickie
- ☐ 1 Hour
- ☐ Tantric
- ☐ BDSM Play
- ☐ Toys
- ☐ All Night Long

WHEN: ☐ Monday ☐ Tuesday ☐ Wednesday ☐ Thursday ☐ Friday ☐ Saturday ☐ Sunday

To Be Paid By _____   Signed _____

Back Side Of Check

Tear Here Across This Line

DATE: _____

SEX CHECK 005

PAY TO THE
ORDER OF: _____

GOING OUT: One Night Of Fun Followed By Sensual Passionate Love

- ☐ Dancing
- ☐ Drinking
- ☐ Movies
- ☐ Bowling
- ☐ Concert
- ☐ Other _____ Write In Your Own

- ☐ Blowjob
- ☐ Eating Out
- ☐ Missionary
- ☐ Doggystyle
- ☐ On top
- ☐ Other _____ Write In Your Own

- ☐ Car
- ☐ Bed
- ☐ Kitchen
- ☐ Hotel
- ☐ Outside
- ☐ Other _____ Write In Your Own

- ☐ Quickie
- ☐ 1 Hour
- ☐ Tantric
- ☐ BDSM Play
- ☐ Toys
- ☐ All Night Long

WHEN: ☐ Monday ☐ Tuesday ☐ Wednesday ☐ Thursday ☐ Friday ☐ Saturday ☐ Sunday

To Be Paid By _____ Signed _____

Back Side Of Check

Tear Here Across This Line

DATE: _____

SEX CHECK 006

PAY TO THE
ORDER OF: _____

GOING OUT: One Night Of Fun Followed By Sensual Passionate Love

- ☐ Dancing
- ☐ Drinking
- ☐ Movies
- ☐ Bowling
- ☐ Concert
- ☐ Other _____ Write In Your Own

- ☐ Blowjob
- ☐ Eating Out
- ☐ Missionary
- ☐ Doggystyle
- ☐ On top
- ☐ Other _____ Write In Your Own

- ☐ Car
- ☐ Bed
- ☐ Kitchen
- ☐ Hotel
- ☐ Outside
- ☐ Other _____ Write In Your Own

- ☐ Quickie
- ☐ 1 Hour
- ☐ Tantric
- ☐ BDSM Play
- ☐ Toys
- ☐ All Night Long

WHEN: ☐ Monday ☐ Tuesday ☐ Wednesday ☐ Thursday ☐ Friday ☐ Saturday ☐ Sunday

To Be Paid By _____ Signed _____

Back Side Of Check

Tear Here Across This Line

SEX CHECK 007

DATE: _____

PAY TO THE
ORDER OF: _____

GOING OUT: One Night Of Fun Followed By Sensual Passionate Love

- ☐ Dancing
- ☐ Drinking
- ☐ Movies
- ☐ Bowling
- ☐ Concert
- ☐ Other _____ Write In Your Own

- ☐ Blowjob
- ☐ Eating Out
- ☐ Missionary
- ☐ Doggystyle
- ☐ On top
- ☐ Other _____ Write In Your Own

- ☐ Car
- ☐ Bed
- ☐ Kitchen
- ☐ Hotel
- ☐ Outside
- ☐ Other _____ Write In Your Own

- ☐ Quickie
- ☐ 1 Hour
- ☐ Tantric
- ☐ BDSM Play
- ☐ Toys
- ☐ All Night Long

WHEN: ☐ Monday ☐ Tuesday ☐ Wednesday ☐ Thursday ☐ Friday ☐ Saturday ☐ Sunday

To Be Paid By _____ Signed _____

Back Side Of Check

Tear Here Across This Line

DATE: _____

SEX CHECK DOB

PAY TO THE
ORDER OF: _____

GOING OUT: One Night Of Fun Followed By Sensual Passionate Love

- ☐ Dancing
- ☐ Drinking
- ☐ Movies
- ☐ Bowling
- ☐ Concert
- ☐ Other _____ Write In Your Own

- ☐ Blowjob
- ☐ Eating Out
- ☐ Missionary
- ☐ Doggystyle
- ☐ On top
- ☐ Other _____ Write In Your Own

- ☐ Car
- ☐ Bed
- ☐ Kitchen
- ☐ Hotel
- ☐ Outside
- ☐ Other _____ Write In Your Own

- ☐ Quickie
- ☐ 1 Hour
- ☐ Tantric
- ☐ BDSM Play
- ☐ Toys
- ☐ All Night Long

WHEN: ☐ Monday ☐ Tuesday ☐ Wednesday ☐ Thursday ☐ Friday ☐ Saturday ☐ Sunday

To Be Paid By _____   Signed _____

Back Side Of Check

Tear Here Across This Line

DATE: _____

SEX CHECK 009

PAY TO THE
ORDER OF: _____

GOING OUT: One Night Of Fun Followed By Sensual Passionate Love

- [ ] Dancing
- [ ] Drinking
- [ ] Movies
- [ ] Bowling
- [ ] Concert
- [ ] Other _____ Write In Your Own

- [ ] Blowjob
- [ ] Eating Out
- [ ] Missionary
- [ ] Doggystyle
- [ ] On top
- [ ] Other _____ Write In Your Own

- [ ] Car
- [ ] Bed
- [ ] Kitchen
- [ ] Hotel
- [ ] Outside
- [ ] Other _____ Write In Your Own

- [ ] Quickie
- [ ] 1 Hour
- [ ] Tantric
- [ ] BDSM Play
- [ ] Toys
- [ ] All Night Long

WHEN:
- [ ] Monday
- [ ] Tuesday
- [ ] Wednesday
- [ ] Thursday
- [ ] Friday
- [ ] Saturday
- [ ] Sunday

To Be Paid By _____   Signed _____

Back Side Of Check

Tear Here Across This Line

DATE: _____

SEX CHECK 01D

PAY TO THE
ORDER OF: _____

GOING OUT: One Night Of Fun Followed By Sensual Passionate Love

- ☐ Dancing
- ☐ Drinking
- ☐ Movies
- ☐ Bowling
- ☐ Concert
- ☐ Other _____ Write In Your Own

- ☐ Blowjob
- ☐ Eating Out
- ☐ Missionary
- ☐ Doggystyle
- ☐ On top
- ☐ Other _____ Write In Your Own

- ☐ Car
- ☐ Bed
- ☐ Kitchen
- ☐ Hotel
- ☐ Outside
- ☐ Other _____ Write In Your Own

- ☐ Quickie
- ☐ 1 Hour
- ☐ Tantric
- ☐ BDSM Play
- ☐ Toys
- ☐ All Night Long

WHEN: ☐ Monday ☐ Tuesday ☐ Wednesday ☐ Thursday ☐ Friday ☐ Saturday ☐ Sunday

To Be Paid By _____   Signed _____

Back Side Of Check

Tear Here Across This Line

DATE: _____

SEX CHECK 011

PAY TO THE
ORDER OF: _____

GOING OUT: One Night Of Fun Followed By Sensual Passionate Love

- ☐ Dancing
- ☐ Drinking
- ☐ Movies
- ☐ Bowling
- ☐ Concert
- ☐ Other _____ Write In Your Own

- ☐ Blowjob
- ☐ Eating Out
- ☐ Missionary
- ☐ Doggystyle
- ☐ On top
- ☐ Other _____ Write In Your Own

- ☐ Car
- ☐ Bed
- ☐ Kitchen
- ☐ Hotel
- ☐ Outside
- ☐ Other _____ Write In Your Own

- ☐ Quickie
- ☐ 1 Hour
- ☐ Tantric
- ☐ BDSM Play
- ☐ Toys
- ☐ All Night Long

WHEN: ☐ Monday ☐ Tuesday ☐ Wednesday ☐ Thursday ☐ Friday ☐ Saturday ☐ Sunday

To Be Paid By _____ Signed _____

Back Side Of Check

Tear Here Across This Line

DATE: _____

SEX CHECK 012

PAY TO THE
ORDER OF: _____

GOING OUT: One Night Of Fun Followed By Sensual Passionate Love

- [ ] Dancing
- [ ] Drinking
- [ ] Movies
- [ ] Bowling
- [ ] Concert
- [ ] Other _____ Write In Your Own

- [ ] Blowjob
- [ ] Eating Out
- [ ] Missionary
- [ ] Doggystyle
- [ ] On top
- [ ] Other _____ Write In Your Own

- [ ] Car
- [ ] Bed
- [ ] Kitchen
- [ ] Hotel
- [ ] Outside
- [ ] Other _____ Write In Your Own

- [ ] Quickie
- [ ] 1 Hour
- [ ] Tantric
- [ ] BDSM Play
- [ ] Toys
- [ ] All Night Long

WHEN: [ ] Monday [ ] Tuesday [ ] Wednesday [ ] Thursday [ ] Friday [ ] Saturday [ ] Sunday

To Be Paid By _____   Signed _____

Back Side Of Check

Tear Here Across This Line

DATE: _____

SEX CHECK 013

PAY TO THE
ORDER OF: _____

GOING OUT: One Night Of Fun Followed By Sensual Passionate Love

- ☐ Dancing
- ☐ Drinking
- ☐ Movies
- ☐ Bowling
- ☐ Concert
- ☐ Other _____ Write In Your Own

- ☐ Blowjob
- ☐ Eating Out
- ☐ Missionary
- ☐ Doggystyle
- ☐ On top
- ☐ Other _____ Write In Your Own

- ☐ Car
- ☐ Bed
- ☐ Kitchen
- ☐ Hotel
- ☐ Outside
- ☐ Other _____ Write In Your Own

- ☐ Quickie
- ☐ 1 Hour
- ☐ Tantric
- ☐ BDSM Play
- ☐ Toys
- ☐ All Night Long

WHEN: ☐ Monday ☐ Tuesday ☐ Wednesday ☐ Thursday ☐ Friday ☐ Saturday ☐ Sunday

To Be Paid By _____   Signed _____

Back Side Of Check

Tear Here Across This Line

DATE: _____

SEX CHECK 014

PAY TO THE
ORDER OF: _____

GOING OUT: One Night Of Fun Followed By Sensual Passionate Love

- ☐ Dancing
- ☐ Drinking
- ☐ Movies
- ☐ Bowling
- ☐ Concert
- ☐ Other _____ Write In Your Own

- ☐ Blowjob
- ☐ Eating Out
- ☐ Missionary
- ☐ Doggystyle
- ☐ On top
- ☐ Other _____ Write In Your Own

- ☐ Car
- ☐ Bed
- ☐ Kitchen
- ☐ Hotel
- ☐ Outside
- ☐ Other _____ Write In Your Own

- ☐ Quickie
- ☐ 1 Hour
- ☐ Tantric
- ☐ BDSM Play
- ☐ Toys
- ☐ All Night Long

WHEN: ☐ Monday ☐ Tuesday ☐ Wednesday ☐ Thursday ☐ Friday ☐ Saturday ☐ Sunday

To Be Paid By _____ Signed _____

Back Side Of Check

Tear Here Across This Line

DATE: _____

SEX CHECK 015

PAY TO THE
ORDER OF: _____

GOING OUT: One Night Of Fun Followed By Sensual Passionate Love

- ☐ Dancing
- ☐ Drinking
- ☐ Movies
- ☐ Bowling
- ☐ Concert
- ☐ Other _____ Write In Your Own

- ☐ Blowjob
- ☐ Eating Out
- ☐ Missionary
- ☐ Doggystyle
- ☐ On top
- ☐ Other _____ Write In Your Own

- ☐ Car
- ☐ Bed
- ☐ Kitchen
- ☐ Hotel
- ☐ Outside
- ☐ Other _____ Write In Your Own

- ☐ Quickie
- ☐ 1 Hour
- ☐ Tantric
- ☐ BDSM Play
- ☐ Toys
- ☐ All Night Long

WHEN: ☐ Monday ☐ Tuesday ☐ Wednesday ☐ Thursday ☐ Friday ☐ Saturday ☐ Sunday

To Be Paid By _____   Signed _____

Back Side Of Check

Tear Here Across This Line

SEX CHECK 01*6*

DATE: _____

PAY TO THE
ORDER OF: _____

GOING OUT: One Night Of Fun Followed By Sensual Passionate Love

- ☐ Dancing
- ☐ Drinking
- ☐ Movies
- ☐ Bowling
- ☐ Concert
- ☐ Other _____ Write In Your Own

- ☐ Blowjob
- ☐ Eating Out
- ☐ Missionary
- ☐ Doggystyle
- ☐ On top
- ☐ Other _____ Write In Your Own

- ☐ Car
- ☐ Bed
- ☐ Kitchen
- ☐ Hotel
- ☐ Outside
- ☐ Other _____ Write In Your Own

- ☐ Quickie
- ☐ 1 Hour
- ☐ Tantric
- ☐ BDSM Play
- ☐ Toys
- ☐ All Night Long

WHEN: ☐ Monday ☐ Tuesday ☐ Wednesday ☐ Thursday ☐ Friday ☐ Saturday ☐ Sunday

To Be Paid By _____   Signed _____

Back Side Of Check

Tear Here Across This Line

DATE: _____

SEX CHECK 017

PAY TO THE
ORDER OF: _____

GOING OUT: One Night Of Fun Followed By Sensual Passionate Love

- ☐ Blowjob
- ☐ Eating Out
- ☐ Missionary
- ☐ Doggystyle
- ☐ On top
- ☐ Other _____ Write In Your Own

- ☐ Car
- ☐ Bed
- ☐ Kitchen
- ☐ Hotel
- ☐ Outside
- ☐ Other _____ Write In Your Own

- ☐ Quickie
- ☐ 1 Hour
- ☐ Tantric
- ☐ BDSM Play
- ☐ Toys
- ☐ All Night Long

- ☐ Dancing
- ☐ Drinking
- ☐ Movies
- ☐ Bowling
- ☐ Concert
- ☐ Other _____ Write In Your Own

WHEN: ☐ Monday ☐ Tuesday ☐ Wednesday ☐ Thursday ☐ Friday ☐ Saturday ☐ Sunday

To Be Paid By _____   Signed _____

BACK SIDE OF CHECK

Tear Here Across This Line

DATE: _____

SEX CHECK 018

PAY TO THE
ORDER OF: _____

GOING OUT: One Night Of Fun Followed By Sensual Passionate Love

- ☐ Dancing
- ☐ Drinking
- ☐ Movies
- ☐ Bowling
- ☐ Concert
- ☐ Other _____ *Write In Your Own*

- ☐ Blowjob
- ☐ Eating Out
- ☐ Missionary
- ☐ Doggystyle
- ☐ On top
- ☐ Other _____ *Write In Your Own*

- ☐ Car
- ☐ Bed
- ☐ Kitchen
- ☐ Hotel
- ☐ Outside
- ☐ Other _____ *Write In Your Own*

- ☐ Quickie
- ☐ 1 Hour
- ☐ Tantric
- ☐ BDSM Play
- ☐ Toys
- ☐ All Night Long

WHEN: ☐ Monday ☐ Tuesday ☐ Wednesday ☐ Thursday ☐ Friday ☐ Saturday ☐ Sunday

To Be Paid By _____   Signed _____

Back Side Of Check

Tear Here Across This Line

DATE: _____

SEX CHECK 019

PAY TO THE
ORDER OF: _____

GOING OUT: One Night Of Fun Followed By Sensual Passionate Love

- ☐ Dancing
- ☐ Drinking
- ☐ Movies
- ☐ Bowling
- ☐ Concert
- ☐ Other _____ Write In Your Own

- ☐ Blowjob
- ☐ Eating Out
- ☐ Missionary
- ☐ Doggystyle
- ☐ On top
- ☐ Other _____ Write In Your Own

- ☐ Car
- ☐ Bed
- ☐ Kitchen
- ☐ Hotel
- ☐ Outside
- ☐ Other _____ Write In Your Own

- ☐ Quickie
- ☐ 1 Hour
- ☐ Tantric
- ☐ BDSM Play
- ☐ Toys
- ☐ All Night Long

WHEN: ☐ Monday ☐ Tuesday ☐ Wednesday ☐ Thursday ☐ Friday ☐ Saturday ☐ Sunday

To Be Paid By _____ Signed _____

Back Side Of Check

Tear Here Across This Line

DATE: _____

SEX CHECK 02D

PAY TO THE
ORDER OF: _____

GOING OUT: One Night Of Fun Followed By Sensual Passionate Love

- [ ] Dancing
- [ ] Drinking
- [ ] Movies
- [ ] Bowling
- [ ] Concert
- [ ] Other _____ Write In Your Own

- [ ] Blowjob
- [ ] Eating Out
- [ ] Missionary
- [ ] Doggystyle
- [ ] On top
- [ ] Other _____ Write In Your Own

- [ ] Car
- [ ] Bed
- [ ] Kitchen
- [ ] Hotel
- [ ] Outside
- [ ] Other _____ Write In Your Own

- [ ] Quickie
- [ ] 1 Hour
- [ ] Tantric
- [ ] BDSM Play
- [ ] Toys
- [ ] All Night Long

WHEN:
- [ ] Monday
- [ ] Tuesday
- [ ] Wednesday
- [ ] Thursday
- [ ] Friday
- [ ] Saturday
- [ ] Sunday

To Be Paid By _____   Signed _____

Back Side Of Check

Tear Here Across This Line

DATE: _____

Sex Check 021

PAY TO THE
ORDER OF: _____

GOING OUT: One Night Of Fun Followed By Sensual Passionate Love

- ☐ Dancing
- ☐ Drinking
- ☐ Movies
- ☐ Bowling
- ☐ Concert
- ☐ Other _____ Write In Your Own

- ☐ Blowjob
- ☐ Eating Out
- ☐ Missionary
- ☐ Doggystyle
- ☐ On top
- ☐ Other _____ Write In Your Own

- ☐ Car
- ☐ Bed
- ☐ Kitchen
- ☐ Hotel
- ☐ Outside
- ☐ Other _____ Write In Your Own

- ☐ Quickie
- ☐ 1 Hour
- ☐ Tantric
- ☐ BDSM Play
- ☐ Toys
- ☐ All Night Long

WHEN: ☐ Monday ☐ Tuesday ☐ Wednesday ☐ Thursday ☐ Friday ☐ Saturday ☐ Sunday

To Be Paid By _____   Signed _____

Back Side Of Check

Tear Here Across This Line

DATE: _____

SEX CHECK 022

PAY TO THE
ORDER OF: _____

GOING OUT: One Night Of Fun Followed By Sensual Passionate Love

- ☐ Dancing
- ☐ Drinking
- ☐ Movies
- ☐ Bowling
- ☐ Concert
- ☐ Other _____ Write In Your Own

- ☐ Blowjob
- ☐ Eating Out
- ☐ Missionary
- ☐ Doggystyle
- ☐ On top
- ☐ Other _____ Write In Your Own

- ☐ Car
- ☐ Bed
- ☐ Kitchen
- ☐ Hotel
- ☐ Outside
- ☐ Other _____ Write In Your Own

- ☐ Quickie
- ☐ 1 Hour
- ☐ Tantric
- ☐ BDSM Play
- ☐ Toys
- ☐ All Night Long

WHEN: ☐ Monday ☐ Tuesday ☐ Wednesday ☐ Thursday ☐ Friday ☐ Saturday ☐ Sunday

To Be Paid By _____ Signed

Back Side Of Check

Tear Here Across This Line

DATE: _____

SEX CHECK D23

PAY TO THE
ORDER OF: _____

GOING OUT: One Night Of Fun Followed By Sensual Passionate Love

- ☐ Dancing
- ☐ Drinking
- ☐ Movies
- ☐ Bowling
- ☐ Concert
- ☐ Other _____ *Write In Your Own*

- ☐ Blowjob
- ☐ Eating Out
- ☐ Missionary
- ☐ Doggystyle
- ☐ On top
- ☐ Other _____ *Write In Your Own*

- ☐ Car
- ☐ Bed
- ☐ Kitchen
- ☐ Hotel
- ☐ Outside
- ☐ Other _____ *Write In Your Own*

- ☐ Quickie
- ☐ 1 Hour
- ☐ Tantric
- ☐ BDSM Play
- ☐ Toys
- ☐ All Night Long

WHEN: ☐ Monday ☐ Tuesday ☐ Wednesday ☐ Thursday ☐ Friday ☐ Saturday ☐ Sunday

To Be Paid By _____

Signed _____

Back Side Of Check

Tear Here Across This Line

DATE: _____

SEX CHECK **024**

PAY TO THE
ORDER OF: _____

GOING OUT: One Night Of Fun Followed By Sensual Passionate Love

- ☐ Dancing
- ☐ Drinking
- ☐ Movies
- ☐ Bowling
- ☐ Concert
- ☐ Other _____ *Write In Your Own*

- ☐ Blowjob
- ☐ Eating Out
- ☐ Missionary
- ☐ Doggystyle
- ☐ On top
- ☐ Other _____ *Write In Your Own*

- ☐ Car
- ☐ Bed
- ☐ Kitchen
- ☐ Hotel
- ☐ Outside
- ☐ Other _____ *Write In Your Own*

- ☐ Quickie
- ☐ 1 Hour
- ☐ Tantric
- ☐ BDSM Play
- ☐ Toys
- ☐ All Night Long

WHEN: ☐ Monday ☐ Tuesday ☐ Wednesday ☐ Thursday ☐ Friday ☐ Saturday ☐ Sunday

To Be Paid By _____   Signed _____

Back Side Of Check

Tear Here Across This Line

DATE: _____

SEX CHECK 025

PAY TO THE
ORDER OF: _____

GOING OUT: One Night Of Fun Followed By Sensual Passionate Love

- ☐ Dancing
- ☐ Drinking
- ☐ Movies
- ☐ Bowling
- ☐ Concert
- ☐ Other _____ *Write In Your Own*

- ☐ Blowjob
- ☐ Eating Out
- ☐ Missionary
- ☐ Doggystyle
- ☐ On top
- ☐ Other _____ *Write In Your Own*

- ☐ Car
- ☐ Bed
- ☐ Kitchen
- ☐ Hotel
- ☐ Outside
- ☐ Other _____ *Write In Your Own*

- ☐ Quickie
- ☐ 1 Hour
- ☐ Tantric
- ☐ BDSM Play
- ☐ Toys
- ☐ All Night Long

WHEN: ☐ Monday ☐ Tuesday ☐ Wednesday ☐ Thursday ☐ Friday ☐ Saturday ☐ Sunday

To Be Paid By _____   Signed _____

Back Side Of Check

Tear Here Across This Line

DATE: _____

SEX CHECK 02b

PAY TO THE
ORDER OF: _____

GOING OUT: One Night Of Fun Followed By Sensual Passionate Love

- ☐ Dancing
- ☐ Drinking
- ☐ Movies
- ☐ Bowling
- ☐ Concert
- ☐ Other _____ *Write In Your Own*

- ☐ Blowjob
- ☐ Eating Out
- ☐ Missionary
- ☐ Doggystyle
- ☐ On top
- ☐ Other _____ *Write In Your Own*

- ☐ Car
- ☐ Bed
- ☐ Kitchen
- ☐ Hotel
- ☐ Outside
- ☐ Other _____ *Write In Your Own*

- ☐ Quickie
- ☐ 1 Hour
- ☐ Tantric
- ☐ BDSM Play
- ☐ Toys
- ☐ All Night Long

WHEN: ☐ Monday ☐ Tuesday ☐ Wednesday ☐ Thursday ☐ Friday ☐ Saturday ☐ Sunday

To Be Paid By _____ Signed _____

Back Side Of Check

Tear Here Across This Line

DATE: _____

SEX CHECK 027

PAY TO THE
ORDER OF: _____

GOING OUT: One Night Of Fun Followed By Sensual Passionate Love

- ☐ Dancing
- ☐ Drinking
- ☐ Movies
- ☐ Bowling
- ☐ Concert
- ☐ Other _____ Write In Your Own

- ☐ Blowjob
- ☐ Eating Out
- ☐ Missionary
- ☐ Doggystyle
- ☐ On top
- ☐ Other _____ Write In Your Own

- ☐ Car
- ☐ Bed
- ☐ Kitchen
- ☐ Hotel
- ☐ Outside
- ☐ Other _____ Write In Your Own

- ☐ Quickie
- ☐ 1 Hour
- ☐ Tantric
- ☐ BDSM Play
- ☐ Toys
- ☐ All Night Long

WHEN: ☐ Monday ☐ Tuesday ☐ Wednesday ☐ Thursday ☐ Friday ☐ Saturday ☐ Sunday

To Be Paid By _____ Signed _____

Back Side Of Check

Tear Here Across This Line

DATE: _____

SEX CHECK 028

PAY TO THE
ORDER OF: _____

GOING OUT: One Night Of Fun Followed By Sensual Passionate Love

- ☐ Dancing
- ☐ Drinking
- ☐ Movies
- ☐ Bowling
- ☐ Concert
- ☐ Other _____ *Write In Your Own*

- ☐ Blowjob
- ☐ Eating Out
- ☐ Missionary
- ☐ Doggystyle
- ☐ On top
- ☐ Other _____ *Write In Your Own*

- ☐ Car
- ☐ Bed
- ☐ Kitchen
- ☐ Hotel
- ☐ Outside
- ☐ Other _____ *Write In Your Own*

- ☐ Quickie
- ☐ 1 Hour
- ☐ Tantric
- ☐ BDSM Play
- ☐ Toys
- ☐ All Night Long

WHEN: ☐ Monday ☐ Tuesday ☐ Wednesday ☐ Thursday ☐ Friday ☐ Saturday ☐ Sunday

To Be Paid By _____ Signed _____

Back Side Of Check

Tear Here Across This Line

DATE: _____

SEX CHECK 029

PAY TO THE
ORDER OF: _____

GOING OUT: One Night Of Fun Followed By Sensual Passionate Love

- ☐ Dancing
- ☐ Drinking
- ☐ Movies
- ☐ Bowling
- ☐ Concert
- ☐ Other _____ *Write In Your Own*

- ☐ Blowjob
- ☐ Eating Out
- ☐ Missionary
- ☐ Doggystyle
- ☐ On top
- ☐ Other _____ *Write In Your Own*

- ☐ Car
- ☐ Bed
- ☐ Kitchen
- ☐ Hotel
- ☐ Outside
- ☐ Other _____ *Write In Your Own*

- ☐ Quickie
- ☐ 1 Hour
- ☐ Tantric
- ☐ BDSM Play
- ☐ Toys
- ☐ All Night Long

WHEN: ☐ Monday ☐ Tuesday ☐ Wednesday ☐ Thursday ☐ Friday ☐ Saturday ☐ Sunday

To Be Paid By _____   Signed _____

Back Side Of Check

Tear Here Across This Line

DATE: _____

Sex Check 030

PAY TO THE
ORDER OF: _____

GOING OUT: One Night Of Fun Followed By Sensual Passionate Love

- ☐ Dancing
- ☐ Drinking
- ☐ Movies
- ☐ Bowling
- ☐ Concert
- ☐ Other _____ Write In Your Own

- ☐ Blowjob
- ☐ Eating Out
- ☐ Missionary
- ☐ Doggystyle
- ☐ On top
- ☐ Other _____ Write In Your Own

- ☐ Car
- ☐ Bed
- ☐ Kitchen
- ☐ Hotel
- ☐ Outside
- ☐ Other _____ Write In Your Own

- ☐ Quickie
- ☐ 1 Hour
- ☐ Tantric
- ☐ BDSM Play
- ☐ Toys
- ☐ All Night Long

WHEN: ☐ Monday ☐ Tuesday ☐ Wednesday ☐ Thursday ☐ Friday ☐ Saturday ☐ Sunday

To Be Paid By

Signed _____

Back Side Of Check

Tear Here Across This Line

DATE: _____

SEX CHECK D31

PAY TO THE
ORDER OF: _____

GOING OUT: One Night Of Fun Followed By Sensual Passionate Love

- ☐ Blowjob
- ☐ Eating Out
- ☐ Missionary
- ☐ Doggystyle
- ☐ On top
- ☐ Other _____ Write In Your Own

- ☐ Car
- ☐ Bed
- ☐ Kitchen
- ☐ Hotel
- ☐ Outside
- ☐ Other _____ Write In Your Own

- ☐ Quickie
- ☐ 1 Hour
- ☐ Tantric
- ☐ BDSM Play
- ☐ Toys
- ☐ All Night Long

- ☐ Dancing
- ☐ Drinking
- ☐ Movies
- ☐ Bowling
- ☐ Concert
- ☐ Other _____ Write In Your Own

WHEN: ☐ Monday ☐ Tuesday ☐ Wednesday ☐ Thursday ☐ Friday ☐ Saturday ☐ Sunday

To Be Paid By _____ Signed _____

Back Side Of Check

Tear Here Across This Line

DATE: _____

SEX CHECK 032

PAY TO THE
ORDER OF: _____

GOING OUT: One Night Of Fun Followed By Sensual Passionate Love

- ☐ Dancing
- ☐ Drinking
- ☐ Movies
- ☐ Bowling
- ☐ Concert
- ☐ Other _____ Write In Your Own

- ☐ Blowjob
- ☐ Eating Out
- ☐ Missionary
- ☐ Doggystyle
- ☐ On top
- ☐ Other _____ Write In Your Own

- ☐ Car
- ☐ Bed
- ☐ Kitchen
- ☐ Hotel
- ☐ Outside
- ☐ Other _____ Write In Your Own

- ☐ Quickie
- ☐ 1 Hour
- ☐ Tantric
- ☐ BDSM Play
- ☐ Toys
- ☐ All Night Long

WHEN: ☐ Monday ☐ Tuesday ☐ Wednesday ☐ Thursday ☐ Friday ☐ Saturday ☐ Sunday

To Be Paid By _____

Signed _____

Back Side Of Check

Tear Here Across This Line

DATE: _____

SEX CHECK 033

PAY TO THE
ORDER OF: _____

GOING OUT: One Night Of Fun Followed By Sensual Passionate Love

- ☐ Dancing
- ☐ Drinking
- ☐ Movies
- ☐ Bowling
- ☐ Concert
- ☐ Other _____ *Write In Your Own*

- ☐ Blowjob
- ☐ Eating Out
- ☐ Missionary
- ☐ Doggystyle
- ☐ On top
- ☐ Other _____ *Write In Your Own*

- ☐ Car
- ☐ Bed
- ☐ Kitchen
- ☐ Hotel
- ☐ Outside
- ☐ Other _____ *Write In Your Own*

- ☐ Quickie
- ☐ 1 Hour
- ☐ Tantric
- ☐ BDSM Play
- ☐ Toys
- ☐ All Night Long

WHEN:
☐ Monday ☐ Tuesday ☐ Wednesday ☐ Thursday ☐ Friday ☐ Saturday ☐ Sunday

To Be Paid By _____   Signed _____

Back Side Of Check

Tear Here Across This Line

DATE: _____

Sex Check D34

PAY TO THE
ORDER OF: _____

GOING OUT: One Night Of Fun Followed By Sensual Passionate Love

- ☐ Blowjob
- ☐ Eating Out
- ☐ Missionary
- ☐ Doggystyle
- ☐ On top
- ☐ Other _____ Write In Your Own

- ☐ Car
- ☐ Bed
- ☐ Kitchen
- ☐ Hotel
- ☐ Outside
- ☐ Other _____ Write In Your Own

- ☐ Quickie
- ☐ 1 Hour
- ☐ Tantric
- ☐ BDSM Play
- ☐ Toys
- ☐ All Night Long

- ☐ Dancing
- ☐ Drinking
- ☐ Movies
- ☐ Bowling
- ☐ Concert
- ☐ Other _____ Write In Your Own

WHEN: ☐ Monday ☐ Tuesday ☐ Wednesday ☐ Thursday ☐ Friday ☐ Saturday ☐ Sunday

To Be Paid By _____ Signed _____

Back Side Of Check

Tear Here Across This Line

DATE: _____

SEX CHECK 035

PAY TO THE
ORDER OF: _____

GOING OUT: One Night Of Fun Followed By Sensual Passionate Love

- ☐ Dancing
- ☐ Drinking
- ☐ Movies
- ☐ Bowling
- ☐ Concert
- ☐ Other _____ _{Write In Your Own}

- ☐ Blowjob
- ☐ Eating Out
- ☐ Missionary
- ☐ Doggystyle
- ☐ On top
- ☐ Other _____ _{Write In Your Own}

- ☐ Car
- ☐ Bed
- ☐ Kitchen
- ☐ Hotel
- ☐ Outside
- ☐ Other _____ _{Write In Your Own}

- ☐ Quickie
- ☐ 1 Hour
- ☐ Tantric
- ☐ BDSM Play
- ☐ Toys
- ☐ All Night Long

WHEN: ☐ Monday ☐ Tuesday ☐ Wednesday ☐ Thursday ☐ Friday ☐ Saturday ☐ Sunday

To Be Paid By

_____
Signed

Back Side Of Check

Tear Here Across This Line

DATE: _____

SEX CHECK D3/6

PAY TO THE
ORDER OF: _____

GOING OUT: One Night Of Fun Followed By Sensual Passionate Love

- ☐ Dancing
- ☐ Drinking
- ☐ Movies
- ☐ Bowling
- ☐ Concert
- ☐ Other _____ Write In Your Own

- ☐ Blowjob
- ☐ Eating Out
- ☐ Missionary
- ☐ Doggystyle
- ☐ On top
- ☐ Other _____ Write In Your Own

- ☐ Car
- ☐ Bed
- ☐ Kitchen
- ☐ Hotel
- ☐ Outside
- ☐ Other _____ Write In Your Own

- ☐ Quickie
- ☐ 1 Hour
- ☐ Tantric
- ☐ BDSM Play
- ☐ Toys
- ☐ All Night Long

WHEN: ☐ Monday ☐ Tuesday ☐ Wednesday ☐ Thursday ☐ Friday ☐ Saturday ☐ Sunday

To Be Paid By _____ Signed _____

Back Side Of Check

Tear Here Across This Line

DATE: _____

SEX CHECK D37

PAY TO THE
ORDER OF: _____

GOING OUT: One Night Of Fun Followed By Sensual Passionate Love

- ☐ Dancing
- ☐ Drinking
- ☐ Movies
- ☐ Bowling
- ☐ Concert
- ☐ Other _____ Write In Your Own

- ☐ Blowjob
- ☐ Eating Out
- ☐ Missionary
- ☐ Doggystyle
- ☐ On top
- ☐ Other _____ Write In Your Own

- ☐ Car
- ☐ Bed
- ☐ Kitchen
- ☐ Hotel
- ☐ Outside
- ☐ Other _____ Write In Your Own

- ☐ Quickie
- ☐ 1 Hour
- ☐ Tantric
- ☐ BDSM Play
- ☐ Toys
- ☐ All Night Long

WHEN: ☐ Monday ☐ Tuesday ☐ Wednesday ☐ Thursday ☐ Friday ☐ Saturday ☐ Sunday

To Be Paid By _____ Signed _____

Back Side Of Check

Tear Here Across This Line

DATE: _____

Sex Check D3B

PAY TO THE
ORDER OF: _____

GOING OUT: One Night Of Fun Followed By Sensual Passionate Love

- ☐ Dancing
- ☐ Drinking
- ☐ Movies
- ☐ Bowling
- ☐ Concert
- ☐ Other _____ Write In Your Own

- ☐ Blowjob
- ☐ Eating Out
- ☐ Missionary
- ☐ Doggystyle
- ☐ On top
- ☐ Other _____ Write In Your Own

- ☐ Car
- ☐ Bed
- ☐ Kitchen
- ☐ Hotel
- ☐ Outside
- ☐ Other _____ Write In Your Own

- ☐ Quickie
- ☐ 1 Hour
- ☐ Tantric
- ☐ BDSM Play
- ☐ Toys
- ☐ All Night Long

WHEN: ☐ Monday ☐ Tuesday ☐ Wednesday ☐ Thursday ☐ Friday ☐ Saturday ☐ Sunday

To Be Paid By _____   Signed _____

Back Side Of Check

Tear Here Across This Line

DATE: _____

Sex Check 039

PAY TO THE
ORDER OF: _____

GOING OUT: One Night Of Fun Followed By Sensual Passionate Love

- ☐ Dancing
- ☐ Drinking
- ☐ Movies
- ☐ Bowling
- ☐ Concert
- ☐ Other _____ Write In Your Own

- ☐ Blowjob
- ☐ Eating Out
- ☐ Missionary
- ☐ Doggystyle
- ☐ On top
- ☐ Other _____ Write In Your Own

- ☐ Car
- ☐ Bed
- ☐ Kitchen
- ☐ Hotel
- ☐ Outside
- ☐ Other _____ Write In Your Own

- ☐ Quickie
- ☐ 1 Hour
- ☐ Tantric
- ☐ BDSM Play
- ☐ Toys
- ☐ All Night Long

WHEN: ☐ Monday ☐ Tuesday ☐ Wednesday ☐ Thursday ☐ Friday ☐ Saturday ☐ Sunday

To Be Paid By _____   Signed _____

Back Side Of Check

Tear Here Across This Line

DATE: _____

SEX CHECK D4D

PAY TO THE
ORDER OF: _____

GOING OUT: One Night Of Fun Followed By Sensual Passionate Love

- ☐ Blowjob
- ☐ Eating Out
- ☐ Missionary
- ☐ Doggystyle
- ☐ On top
- ☐ Other _____ Write In Your Own

- ☐ Car
- ☐ Bed
- ☐ Kitchen
- ☐ Hotel
- ☐ Outside
- ☐ Other _____ Write In Your Own

- ☐ Quickie
- ☐ 1 Hour
- ☐ Tantric
- ☐ BDSM Play
- ☐ Toys
- ☐ All Night Long

- ☐ Dancing
- ☐ Drinking
- ☐ Movies
- ☐ Bowling
- ☐ Concert
- ☐ Other _____ Write In Your Own

WHEN: ☐ Monday ☐ Tuesday ☐ Wednesday ☐ Thursday ☐ Friday ☐ Saturday ☐ Sunday

To Be Paid By _____   Signed _____

Back Side Of Check

Tear Here Across This Line

DATE: _____

S<small>EX</small> C<small>HECK</small> 041

PAY TO THE
ORDER OF: _____

GOING OUT: One Night Of Fun Followed By Sensual Passionate Love

- ☐ Dancing
- ☐ Drinking
- ☐ Movies
- ☐ Bowling
- ☐ Concert
- ☐ Other _____ Write In Your Own

- ☐ Blowjob
- ☐ Eating Out
- ☐ Missionary
- ☐ Doggystyle
- ☐ On top
- ☐ Other _____ Write In Your Own

- ☐ Car
- ☐ Bed
- ☐ Kitchen
- ☐ Hotel
- ☐ Outside
- ☐ Other _____ Write In Your Own

- ☐ Quickie
- ☐ 1 Hour
- ☐ Tantric
- ☐ BDSM Play
- ☐ Toys
- ☐ All Night Long

WHEN: ☐ Monday ☐ Tuesday ☐ Wednesday ☐ Thursday ☐ Friday ☐ Saturday ☐ Sunday

To Be Paid By _____   Signed _____

Back Side Of Check

Tear Here Across This Line

DATE: _____

SEX CHECK **042**

PAY TO THE
ORDER OF: _____

GOING OUT: One Night Of Fun Followed By Sensual Passionate Love

- ☐ Dancing
- ☐ Drinking
- ☐ Movies
- ☐ Bowling
- ☐ Concert
- ☐ Other _____ *Write In Your Own*

- ☐ Blowjob
- ☐ Eating Out
- ☐ Missionary
- ☐ Doggystyle
- ☐ On top
- ☐ Other _____ *Write In Your Own*

- ☐ Car
- ☐ Bed
- ☐ Kitchen
- ☐ Hotel
- ☐ Outside
- ☐ Other _____ *Write In Your Own*

- ☐ Quickie
- ☐ 1 Hour
- ☐ Tantric
- ☐ BDSM Play
- ☐ Toys
- ☐ All Night Long

WHEN: ☐ Monday ☐ Tuesday ☐ Wednesday ☐ Thursday ☐ Friday ☐ Saturday ☐ Sunday

To Be Paid By _____ Signed _____

Back Side Of Check

Tear Here Across This Line

DATE: _____

Sex Check 043

PAY TO THE
ORDER OF: _____

GOING OUT: One Night Of Fun Followed By Sensual Passionate Love

- ☐ Dancing
- ☐ Drinking
- ☐ Movies
- ☐ Bowling
- ☐ Concert
- ☐ Other _____ *Write In Your Own*

- ☐ Blowjob
- ☐ Eating Out
- ☐ Missionary
- ☐ Doggystyle
- ☐ On top
- ☐ Other _____ *Write In Your Own*

- ☐ Car
- ☐ Bed
- ☐ Kitchen
- ☐ Hotel
- ☐ Outside
- ☐ Other _____ *Write In Your Own*

- ☐ Quickie
- ☐ 1 Hour
- ☐ Tantric
- ☐ BDSM Play
- ☐ Toys
- ☐ All Night Long

WHEN: ☐ Monday ☐ Tuesday ☐ Wednesday ☐ Thursday ☐ Friday ☐ Saturday ☐ Sunday

To Be Paid By _____ Signed _____

Back Side Of Check

Tear Here Across This Line

DATE: _____

SEX CHECK 044

PAY TO THE
ORDER OF: _____

GOING OUT: One Night Of Fun Followed By Sensual Passionate Love

- ☐ Dancing
- ☐ Drinking
- ☐ Movies
- ☐ Bowling
- ☐ Concert
- ☐ Other _____ Write In Your Own

- ☐ Blowjob
- ☐ Eating Out
- ☐ Missionary
- ☐ Doggystyle
- ☐ On top
- ☐ Other _____ Write In Your Own

- ☐ Car
- ☐ Bed
- ☐ Kitchen
- ☐ Hotel
- ☐ Outside
- ☐ Other _____ Write In Your Own

- ☐ Quickie
- ☐ 1 Hour
- ☐ Tantric
- ☐ BDSM Play
- ☐ Toys
- ☐ All Night Long

WHEN: ☐ Monday ☐ Tuesday ☐ Wednesday ☐ Thursday ☐ Friday ☐ Saturday ☐ Sunday

To Be Paid By _____   Signed _____

Back Side Of Check

Tear Here Across This Line

DATE: _____

Sex Check 045

PAY TO THE
ORDER OF: _____

GOING OUT: One Night Of Fun Followed By Sensual Passionate Love

- ☐ Dancing
- ☐ Drinking
- ☐ Movies
- ☐ Bowling
- ☐ Concert
- ☐ Other _____ *Write In Your Own*

- ☐ Blowjob
- ☐ Eating Out
- ☐ Missionary
- ☐ Doggystyle
- ☐ On top
- ☐ Other _____ *Write In Your Own*

- ☐ Car
- ☐ Bed
- ☐ Kitchen
- ☐ Hotel
- ☐ Outside
- ☐ Other _____ *Write In Your Own*

- ☐ Quickie
- ☐ 1 Hour
- ☐ Tantric
- ☐ BDSM Play
- ☐ Toys
- ☐ All Night Long

WHEN: ☐ Monday ☐ Tuesday ☐ Wednesday ☐ Thursday ☐ Friday ☐ Saturday ☐ Sunday

To Be Paid By _____

Signed _____

Back Side Of Check

Tear Here Across This Line

DATE: _____

SEX CHECK D4/6

PAY TO THE
ORDER OF: _____

GOING OUT: One Night Of Fun Followed By Sensual Passionate Love

- ☐ Dancing
- ☐ Drinking
- ☐ Movies
- ☐ Bowling
- ☐ Concert
- ☐ Other _____ Write In Your Own

- ☐ Blowjob
- ☐ Eating Out
- ☐ Missionary
- ☐ Doggystyle
- ☐ On top
- ☐ Other _____ Write In Your Own

- ☐ Car
- ☐ Bed
- ☐ Kitchen
- ☐ Hotel
- ☐ Outside
- ☐ Other _____ Write In Your Own

- ☐ Quickie
- ☐ 1 Hour
- ☐ Tantric
- ☐ BDSM Play
- ☐ Toys
- ☐ All Night Long

WHEN: ☐ Monday ☐ Tuesday ☐ Wednesday ☐ Thursday ☐ Friday ☐ Saturday ☐ Sunday

To Be Paid By _____   Signed _____

Back Side Of Check

Tear Here Across This Line

DATE: _____

Sex Check 047

PAY TO THE
ORDER OF: _____

GOING OUT: One Night Of Fun Followed By Sensual Passionate Love

- ☐ Dancing
- ☐ Drinking
- ☐ Movies
- ☐ Bowling
- ☐ Concert
- ☐ Other _____ *Write In Your Own*

- ☐ Blowjob
- ☐ Eating Out
- ☐ Missionary
- ☐ Doggystyle
- ☐ On top
- ☐ Other _____ *Write In Your Own*

- ☐ Car
- ☐ Bed
- ☐ Kitchen
- ☐ Hotel
- ☐ Outside
- ☐ Other _____ *Write In Your Own*

- ☐ Quickie
- ☐ 1 Hour
- ☐ Tantric
- ☐ BDSM Play
- ☐ Toys
- ☐ All Night Long

WHEN: ☐ Monday ☐ Tuesday ☐ Wednesday ☐ Thursday ☐ Friday ☐ Saturday ☐ Sunday

To Be Paid By _____ Signed _____

Back Side Of Check

Tear Here Across This Line

DATE: _____

SEX CHECK 04B

PAY TO THE
ORDER OF: _____

GOING OUT: One Night Of Fun Followed By Sensual Passionate Love

- ☐ Dancing
- ☐ Drinking
- ☐ Movies
- ☐ Bowling
- ☐ Concert
- ☐ Other _____ *Write In Your Own*

- ☐ Blowjob
- ☐ Eating Out
- ☐ Missionary
- ☐ Doggystyle
- ☐ On top
- ☐ Other _____ *Write In Your Own*

- ☐ Car
- ☐ Bed
- ☐ Kitchen
- ☐ Hotel
- ☐ Outside
- ☐ Other _____ *Write In Your Own*

- ☐ Quickie
- ☐ 1 Hour
- ☐ Tantric
- ☐ BDSM Play
- ☐ Toys
- ☐ All Night Long

WHEN: ☐ Monday ☐ Tuesday ☐ Wednesday ☐ Thursday ☐ Friday ☐ Saturday ☐ Sunday

To Be Paid By _____ Signed _____

BACK SIDE OF CHECK

Tear Here Across This Line

DATE: _____

SEX CHECK 049

PAY TO THE
ORDER OF: _____

GOING OUT: One Night Of Fun Followed By Sensual Passionate Love

- ☐ Dancing
- ☐ Drinking
- ☐ Movies
- ☐ Bowling
- ☐ Concert
- ☐ Other _____ *Write In Your Own*

- ☐ Blowjob
- ☐ Eating Out
- ☐ Missionary
- ☐ Doggystyle
- ☐ On top
- ☐ Other _____ *Write In Your Own*

- ☐ Car
- ☐ Bed
- ☐ Kitchen
- ☐ Hotel
- ☐ Outside
- ☐ Other _____ *Write In Your Own*

- ☐ Quickie
- ☐ 1 Hour
- ☐ Tantric
- ☐ BDSM Play
- ☐ Toys
- ☐ All Night Long

WHEN: ☐ Monday ☐ Tuesday ☐ Wednesday ☐ Thursday ☐ Friday ☐ Saturday ☐ Sunday

To Be Paid By _____   Signed _____

Back Side Of Check

Tear Here Across This Line

DATE: _____

SEX CHECK

PAY TO THE
ORDER OF: _____

GOING OUT: One Night Of Fun Followed By Sensual Passionate Love

- ☐ Dancing
- ☐ Drinking
- ☐ Movies
- ☐ Bowling
- ☐ Concert
- ☐ Other _____ Write In Your Own

- ☐ Blowjob
- ☐ Eating Out
- ☐ Missionary
- ☐ Doggystyle
- ☐ On top
- ☐ Other _____ Write In Your Own

- ☐ Car
- ☐ Bed
- ☐ Kitchen
- ☐ Hotel
- ☐ Outside
- ☐ Other _____ Write In Your Own

- ☐ Quickie
- ☐ 1 Hour
- ☐ Tantric
- ☐ BDSM Play
- ☐ Toys
- ☐ All Night Long

WHEN: ☐ Monday ☐ Tuesday ☐ Wednesday ☐ Thursday ☐ Friday ☐ Saturday ☐ Sunday

To Be Paid By _____ Signed _____

Back Side Of Check

Second Set of 50 Checks

Tear Here Across This Line

DATE: _____

Sex Check 001

PAY TO THE
ORDER OF: _____

GOING OUT: One Night Of Fun Followed By Sensual Passionate Love

- ☐ Dancing
- ☐ Drinking
- ☐ Movies
- ☐ Bowling
- ☐ Concert
- ☐ Other _____ Write In Your Own

- ☐ Blowjob
- ☐ Eating Out
- ☐ Missionary
- ☐ Doggystyle
- ☐ On top
- ☐ Other _____ Write In Your Own

- ☐ Car
- ☐ Bed
- ☐ Kitchen
- ☐ Hotel
- ☐ Outside
- ☐ Other _____ Write In Your Own

- ☐ Quickie
- ☐ 1 Hour
- ☐ Tantric
- ☐ BDSM Play
- ☐ Toys
- ☐ All Night Long

WHEN: ☐ Monday ☐ Tuesday ☐ Wednesday ☐ Thursday ☐ Friday ☐ Saturday ☐ Sunday

To Be Paid By _____ Signed _____

Back Side Of Check

Tear Here Across This Line

DATE: _____

SEX CHECK 002

PAY TO THE
ORDER OF: _____

GOING OUT: One Night Of Fun Followed By Sensual Passionate Love

- ☐ Dancing
- ☐ Drinking
- ☐ Movies
- ☐ Bowling
- ☐ Concert
- ☐ Other _____ Write In Your Own

- ☐ Blowjob
- ☐ Eating Out
- ☐ Missionary
- ☐ Doggystyle
- ☐ On top
- ☐ Other _____ Write In Your Own

- ☐ Car
- ☐ Bed
- ☐ Kitchen
- ☐ Hotel
- ☐ Outside
- ☐ Other _____ Write In Your Own

- ☐ Quickie
- ☐ 1 Hour
- ☐ Tantric
- ☐ BDSM Play
- ☐ Toys
- ☐ All Night Long

WHEN! ☐ Monday ☐ Tuesday ☐ Wednesday ☐ Thursday ☐ Friday ☐ Saturday ☐ Sunday

To Be Paid By _____   Signed _____

Back Side Of Check

Tear Here Across This Line

DATE: _____

Sex Check 003

PAY TO THE
ORDER OF: _____

GOING OUT: One Night Of Fun Followed By Sensual Passionate Love

- ☐ Dancing
- ☐ Drinking
- ☐ Movies
- ☐ Bowling
- ☐ Concert
- ☐ Other _____ Write In Your Own

- ☐ Blowjob
- ☐ Eating Out
- ☐ Missionary
- ☐ Doggystyle
- ☐ On top
- ☐ Other _____ Write In Your Own

- ☐ Car
- ☐ Bed
- ☐ Kitchen
- ☐ Hotel
- ☐ Outside
- ☐ Other _____ Write In Your Own

- ☐ Quickie
- ☐ 1 Hour
- ☐ Tantric
- ☐ BDSM Play
- ☐ Toys
- ☐ All Night Long

WHEN: ☐ Monday ☐ Tuesday ☐ Wednesday ☐ Thursday ☐ Friday ☐ Saturday ☐ Sunday

To Be Paid By _____   Signed _____

Back Side Of Check

Tear Here Across This Line

DATE: _____

SEX CHECK DD4

PAY TO THE
ORDER OF: _____

GOING OUT: One Night Of Fun Followed By Sensual Passionate Love

- ☐ Dancing
- ☐ Drinking
- ☐ Movies
- ☐ Bowling
- ☐ Concert
- ☐ Other _____ Write In Your Own

- ☐ Blowjob
- ☐ Eating Out
- ☐ Missionary
- ☐ Doggystyle
- ☐ On top
- ☐ Other _____ Write In Your Own

- ☐ Car
- ☐ Bed
- ☐ Kitchen
- ☐ Hotel
- ☐ Outside
- ☐ Other _____ Write In Your Own

- ☐ Quickie
- ☐ 1 Hour
- ☐ Tantric
- ☐ BDSM Play
- ☐ Toys
- ☐ All Night Long

WHEN: ☐ Monday ☐ Tuesday ☐ Wednesday ☐ Thursday ☐ Friday ☐ Saturday ☐ Sunday

To Be Paid By _____   Signed _____

Back Side Of Check

Tear Here Across This Line

DATE: _____

SEX CHECK 005

PAY TO THE
ORDER OF: _____

GOING OUT: One Night Of Fun Followed By Sensual Passionate Love

- ☐ Dancing
- ☐ Drinking
- ☐ Movies
- ☐ Bowling
- ☐ Concert
- ☐ Other _____ Write In Your Own

- ☐ Blowjob
- ☐ Eating Out
- ☐ Missionary
- ☐ Doggystyle
- ☐ On top
- ☐ Other _____ Write In Your Own

- ☐ Car
- ☐ Bed
- ☐ Kitchen
- ☐ Hotel
- ☐ Outside
- ☐ Other _____ Write In Your Own

- ☐ Quickie
- ☐ 1 Hour
- ☐ Tantric
- ☐ BDSM Play
- ☐ Toys
- ☐ All Night Long

WHEN: ☐ Monday ☐ Tuesday ☐ Wednesday ☐ Thursday ☐ Friday ☐ Saturday ☐ Sunday

To Be Paid By _____   Signed _____

Back Side Of Check

Tear Here Across This Line

DATE: _____

SEX CHECK 006

PAY TO THE
ORDER OF: _____

GOING OUT: One Night Of Fun Followed By Sensual Passionate Love

- ☐ Dancing
- ☐ Drinking
- ☐ Movies
- ☐ Bowling
- ☐ Concert
- ☐ Other _____ Write In Your Own

- ☐ Blowjob
- ☐ Eating Out
- ☐ Missionary
- ☐ Doggystyle
- ☐ On top
- ☐ Other _____ Write In Your Own

- ☐ Car
- ☐ Bed
- ☐ Kitchen
- ☐ Hotel
- ☐ Outside
- ☐ Other _____ Write In Your Own

- ☐ Quickie
- ☐ 1 Hour
- ☐ Tantric
- ☐ BDSM Play
- ☐ Toys
- ☐ All Night Long

WHEN: ☐ Monday ☐ Tuesday ☐ Wednesday ☐ Thursday ☐ Friday ☐ Saturday ☐ Sunday

To Be Paid By _____ Signed _____

Back Side Of Check

Tear Here Across This Line

SEX CHECK 007

DATE: _____

PAY TO THE
ORDER OF: _____

GOING OUT: One Night Of Fun Followed By Sensual Passionate Love

- ☐ Dancing
- ☐ Drinking
- ☐ Movies
- ☐ Bowling
- ☐ Concert
- ☐ Other _____ Write In Your Own

- ☐ Blowjob
- ☐ Eating Out
- ☐ Missionary
- ☐ Doggystyle
- ☐ On top
- ☐ Other _____ Write In Your Own

- ☐ Car
- ☐ Bed
- ☐ Kitchen
- ☐ Hotel
- ☐ Outside
- ☐ Other _____ Write In Your Own

- ☐ Quickie
- ☐ 1 Hour
- ☐ Tantric
- ☐ BDSM Play
- ☐ Toys
- ☐ All Night Long

WHEN: ☐ Monday ☐ Tuesday ☐ Wednesday ☐ Thursday ☐ Friday ☐ Saturday ☐ Sunday

To Be Paid By _____   Signed _____

Back Side Of Check

Tear Here Across This Line

DATE: _____

Sex Check 008

PAY TO THE
ORDER OF: _____

GOING OUT: One Night Of Fun Followed By Sensual Passionate Love

- ☐ Dancing
- ☐ Drinking
- ☐ Movies
- ☐ Bowling
- ☐ Concert
- ☐ Other _____ Write In Your Own

- ☐ Blowjob
- ☐ Eating Out
- ☐ Missionary
- ☐ Doggystyle
- ☐ On top
- ☐ Other _____ Write In Your Own

- ☐ Car
- ☐ Bed
- ☐ Kitchen
- ☐ Hotel
- ☐ Outside
- ☐ Other _____ Write In Your Own

- ☐ Quickie
- ☐ 1 Hour
- ☐ Tantric
- ☐ BDSM Play
- ☐ Toys
- ☐ All Night Long

WHEN: ☐ Monday ☐ Tuesday ☐ Wednesday ☐ Thursday ☐ Friday ☐ Saturday ☐ Sunday

To Be Paid By _____   Signed _____

Back Side Of Check

Tear Here Across This Line

DATE: _____

SEX CHECK 009

PAY TO THE
ORDER OF: _____

GOING OUT: One Night Of Fun Followed By Sensual Passionate Love

- ☐ Dancing
- ☐ Drinking
- ☐ Movies
- ☐ Bowling
- ☐ Concert
- ☐ Other _____ Write In Your Own

- ☐ Blowjob
- ☐ Eating Out
- ☐ Missionary
- ☐ Doggystyle
- ☐ On top
- ☐ Other _____ Write In Your Own

- ☐ Car
- ☐ Bed
- ☐ Kitchen
- ☐ Hotel
- ☐ Outside
- ☐ Other _____ Write In Your Own

- ☐ Quickie
- ☐ 1 Hour
- ☐ Tantric
- ☐ BDSM Play
- ☐ Toys
- ☐ All Night Long

WHEN: ☐ Monday ☐ Tuesday ☐ Wednesday ☐ Thursday ☐ Friday ☐ Saturday ☐ Sunday

To Be Paid By _____   Signed _____

Back Side Of Check

Tear Here Across This Line

DATE: _____

SEX CHECK 01D

PAY TO THE
ORDER OF: _____

GOING OUT: One Night Of Fun Followed By Sensual Passionate Love

- ☐ Dancing
- ☐ Drinking
- ☐ Movies
- ☐ Bowling
- ☐ Concert
- ☐ Other _____ Write In Your Own

- ☐ Blowjob
- ☐ Eating Out
- ☐ Missionary
- ☐ Doggystyle
- ☐ On top
- ☐ Other _____ Write In Your Own

- ☐ Car
- ☐ Bed
- ☐ Kitchen
- ☐ Hotel
- ☐ Outside
- ☐ Other _____ Write In Your Own

- ☐ Quickie
- ☐ 1 Hour
- ☐ Tantric
- ☐ BDSM Play
- ☐ Toys
- ☐ All Night Long

WHEN: ☐ Monday ☐ Tuesday ☐ Wednesday ☐ Thursday ☐ Friday ☐ Saturday ☐ Sunday

To Be Paid By _____ Signed _____

Back Side Of Check

Tear Here Across This Line

DATE: _____

SEX CHECK 011

PAY TO THE
ORDER OF: _____

GOING OUT: One Night Of Fun Followed By Sensual Passionate Love

- ☐ Dancing
- ☐ Drinking
- ☐ Movies
- ☐ Bowling
- ☐ Concert
- ☐ Other _____ *Write In Your Own*

- ☐ Blowjob
- ☐ Eating Out
- ☐ Missionary
- ☐ Doggystyle
- ☐ On top
- ☐ Other _____ *Write In Your Own*

- ☐ Car
- ☐ Bed
- ☐ Kitchen
- ☐ Hotel
- ☐ Outside
- ☐ Other _____ *Write In Your Own*

- ☐ Quickie
- ☐ 1 Hour
- ☐ Tantric
- ☐ BDSM Play
- ☐ Toys
- ☐ All Night Long

WHEN: ☐ Monday ☐ Tuesday ☐ Wednesday ☐ Thursday ☐ Friday ☐ Saturday ☐ Sunday

To Be Paid By _____

Signed _____

BACK SIDE OF CHECK

Tear Here Across This Line

DATE: _____

S̲ex C̲heck 012

PAY TO THE
ORDER OF: _____

𝔊𝔒𝔌𝔑𝔊 𝔒𝔘𝔗: One Night Of Fun Followed By Sensual Passionate Love

- ☐ Dancing
- ☐ Drinking
- ☐ Movies
- ☐ Bowling
- ☐ Concert
- ☐ Other _____ Write In Your Own

- ☐ Blowjob
- ☐ Eating Out
- ☐ Missionary
- ☐ Doggystyle
- ☐ On top
- ☐ Other _____ Write In Your Own

- ☐ Car
- ☐ Bed
- ☐ Kitchen
- ☐ Hotel
- ☐ Outside
- ☐ Other _____ Write In Your Own

- ☐ Quickie
- ☐ 1 Hour
- ☐ Tantric
- ☐ BDSM Play
- ☐ Toys
- ☐ All Night Long

W̲hen: ☐ Monday ☐ Tuesday ☐ Wednesday ☐ Thursday ☐ Friday ☐ Saturday ☐ Sunday

To Be Paid By _____   Signed _____

Back Side Of Check

Tear Here Across This Line

DATE: _____

Sex Check 013

PAY TO THE
ORDER OF: _____

GOING OUT: One Night Of Fun Followed By Sensual Passionate Love

- ☐ Dancing
- ☐ Drinking
- ☐ Movies
- ☐ Bowling
- ☐ Concert
- ☐ Other _____ *Write In Your Own*

- ☐ Blowjob
- ☐ Eating Out
- ☐ Missionary
- ☐ Doggystyle
- ☐ On top
- ☐ Other _____ *Write In Your Own*

- ☐ Car
- ☐ Bed
- ☐ Kitchen
- ☐ Hotel
- ☐ Outside
- ☐ Other _____ *Write In Your Own*

- ☐ Quickie
- ☐ 1 Hour
- ☐ Tantric
- ☐ BDSM Play
- ☐ Toys
- ☐ All Night Long

WHEN: ☐ Monday ☐ Tuesday ☐ Wednesday ☐ Thursday ☐ Friday ☐ Saturday ☐ Sunday

To Be Paid By _____   Signed _____

Back Side Of Check

Tear Here Across This Line

DATE: _____

SEX CHECK 014

PAY TO THE
ORDER OF: _____

GOING OUT: One Night Of Fun Followed By Sensual Passionate Love

- ☐ Dancing
- ☐ Drinking
- ☐ Movies
- ☐ Bowling
- ☐ Concert
- ☐ Other _____ Write In Your Own

- ☐ Blowjob
- ☐ Eating Out
- ☐ Missionary
- ☐ Doggystyle
- ☐ On top
- ☐ Other _____ Write In Your Own

- ☐ Car
- ☐ Bed
- ☐ Kitchen
- ☐ Hotel
- ☐ Outside
- ☐ Other _____ Write In Your Own

- ☐ Quickie
- ☐ 1 Hour
- ☐ Tantric
- ☐ BDSM Play
- ☐ Toys
- ☐ All Night Long

WHEN: ☐ Monday ☐ Tuesday ☐ Wednesday ☐ Thursday ☐ Friday ☐ Saturday ☐ Sunday

To Be Paid By _____   Signed _____

Back Side Of Check

Tear Here Across This Line

DATE: _____

SEX CHECK 015

PAY TO THE
ORDER OF: _____

GOING OUT: One Night Of Fun Followed By Sensual Passionate Love

- ☐ Dancing
- ☐ Drinking
- ☐ Movies
- ☐ Bowling
- ☐ Concert
- ☐ Other _____ Write In Your Own

- ☐ Blowjob
- ☐ Eating Out
- ☐ Missionary
- ☐ Doggystyle
- ☐ On top
- ☐ Other _____ Write In Your Own

- ☐ Car
- ☐ Bed
- ☐ Kitchen
- ☐ Hotel
- ☐ Outside
- ☐ Other _____ Write In Your Own

- ☐ Quickie
- ☐ 1 Hour
- ☐ Tantric
- ☐ BDSM Play
- ☐ Toys
- ☐ All Night Long

WHEN: ☐ Monday ☐ Tuesday ☐ Wednesday ☐ Thursday ☐ Friday ☐ Saturday ☐ Sunday

To Be Paid By _____ Signed _____

Back Side Of Check

Tear Here Across This Line

DATE: _____

SEX CHECK 016

PAY TO THE
ORDER OF: _____

GOING OUT: One Night Of Fun Followed By Sensual Passionate Love

- ☐ Dancing
- ☐ Drinking
- ☐ Movies
- ☐ Bowling
- ☐ Concert
- ☐ Other _____ Write In Your Own

- ☐ Blowjob
- ☐ Eating Out
- ☐ Missionary
- ☐ Doggystyle
- ☐ On top
- ☐ Other _____ Write In Your Own

- ☐ Car
- ☐ Bed
- ☐ Kitchen
- ☐ Hotel
- ☐ Outside
- ☐ Other _____ Write In Your Own

- ☐ Quickie
- ☐ 1 Hour
- ☐ Tantric
- ☐ BDSM Play
- ☐ Toys
- ☐ All Night Long

WHEN: ☐ Monday ☐ Tuesday ☐ Wednesday ☐ Thursday ☐ Friday ☐ Saturday ☐ Sunday

To Be Paid By _____   Signed _____

Back Side Of Check

Tear Here Across This Line

DATE: _____

SEX CHECK 017

PAY TO THE
ORDER OF: _____

GOING OUT: One Night Of Fun Followed By Sensual Passionate Love

- [ ] Dancing
- [ ] Drinking
- [ ] Movies
- [ ] Bowling
- [ ] Concert
- [ ] Other _____ *Write In Your Own*

- [ ] Blowjob
- [ ] Eating Out
- [ ] Missionary
- [ ] Doggystyle
- [ ] On top
- [ ] Other _____ *Write In Your Own*

- [ ] Car
- [ ] Bed
- [ ] Kitchen
- [ ] Hotel
- [ ] Outside
- [ ] Other _____ *Write In Your Own*

- [ ] Quickie
- [ ] 1 Hour
- [ ] Tantric
- [ ] BDSM Play
- [ ] Toys
- [ ] All Night Long

WHEN: ☐ Monday ☐ Tuesday ☐ Wednesday ☐ Thursday ☐ Friday ☐ Saturday ☐ Sunday

To Be Paid By _____   Signed _____

Back Side Of Check

Tear Here Across This Line

DATE: _____

Sex Check D18

PAY TO THE
ORDER OF: _____

GOING OUT: One Night Of Fun Followed By Sensual Passionate Love

- ☐ Dancing
- ☐ Drinking
- ☐ Movies
- ☐ Bowling
- ☐ Concert
- ☐ Other _____ Write In Your Own

- ☐ Blowjob
- ☐ Eating Out
- ☐ Missionary
- ☐ Doggystyle
- ☐ On top
- ☐ Other _____ Write In Your Own

- ☐ Car
- ☐ Bed
- ☐ Kitchen
- ☐ Hotel
- ☐ Outside
- ☐ Other _____ Write In Your Own

- ☐ Quickie
- ☐ 1 Hour
- ☐ Tantric
- ☐ BDSM Play
- ☐ Toys
- ☐ All Night Long

WHEN: ☐ Monday ☐ Tuesday ☐ Wednesday ☐ Thursday ☐ Friday ☐ Saturday ☐ Sunday

To Be Paid By _____ Signed _____

Back Side Of Check

Tear Here Across This Line

DATE: _____

Sex Check 019

PAY TO THE
ORDER OF: _____

GOING OUT: One Night Of Fun Followed By Sensual Passionate Love

- ☐ Dancing
- ☐ Drinking
- ☐ Movies
- ☐ Bowling
- ☐ Concert
- ☐ Other _____ Write In Your Own

- ☐ Blowjob
- ☐ Eating Out
- ☐ Missionary
- ☐ Doggystyle
- ☐ On top
- ☐ Other _____ Write In Your Own

- ☐ Car
- ☐ Bed
- ☐ Kitchen
- ☐ Hotel
- ☐ Outside
- ☐ Other _____ Write In Your Own

- ☐ Quickie
- ☐ 1 Hour
- ☐ Tantric
- ☐ BDSM Play
- ☐ Toys
- ☐ All Night Long

WHEN: ☐ Monday ☐ Tuesday ☐ Wednesday ☐ Thursday ☐ Friday ☐ Saturday ☐ Sunday

To Be Paid By _____   Signed _____

Back Side Of Check

Tear Here Across This Line

DATE: _____

SEX CHECK 020

PAY TO THE
ORDER OF: _____

GOING OUT: One Night Of Fun Followed By Sensual Passionate Love

- ☐ Dancing
- ☐ Drinking
- ☐ Movies
- ☐ Bowling
- ☐ Concert
- ☐ Other _____ *Write In Your Own*

- ☐ Blowjob
- ☐ Eating Out
- ☐ Missionary
- ☐ Doggystyle
- ☐ On top
- ☐ Other _____ *Write In Your Own*

- ☐ Car
- ☐ Bed
- ☐ Kitchen
- ☐ Hotel
- ☐ Outside
- ☐ Other _____ *Write In Your Own*

- ☐ Quickie
- ☐ 1 Hour
- ☐ Tantric
- ☐ BDSM Play
- ☐ Toys
- ☐ All Night Long

WHEN: ☐ Monday ☐ Tuesday ☐ Wednesday ☐ Thursday ☐ Friday ☐ Saturday ☐ Sunday

To Be Paid By _____ Signed _____

Back Side Of Check

Tear Here Across This Line

DATE: _____

Sex Check 021

PAY TO THE
ORDER OF: _____

GOING OUT: One Night Of Fun Followed By Sensual Passionate Love

- ☐ Dancing
- ☐ Drinking
- ☐ Movies
- ☐ Bowling
- ☐ Concert
- ☐ Other _____ Write In Your Own

- ☐ Blowjob
- ☐ Eating Out
- ☐ Missionary
- ☐ Doggystyle
- ☐ On top
- ☐ Other _____ Write In Your Own

- ☐ Car
- ☐ Bed
- ☐ Kitchen
- ☐ Hotel
- ☐ Outside
- ☐ Other _____ Write In Your Own

- ☐ Quickie
- ☐ 1 Hour
- ☐ Tantric
- ☐ BDSM Play
- ☐ Toys
- ☐ All Night Long

WHEN: ☐ Monday ☐ Tuesday ☐ Wednesday ☐ Thursday ☐ Friday ☐ Saturday ☐ Sunday

To Be Paid By _____   Signed _____

BACK SIDE OF CHECK

Tear Here Across This Line

SEX CHECK 022

DATE: _____

PAY TO THE
ORDER OF: _____

GOING OUT: One Night Of Fun Followed By Sensual Passionate Love

- ☐ Dancing
- ☐ Drinking
- ☐ Movies
- ☐ Bowling
- ☐ Concert
- ☐ Other _____ Write In Your Own

- ☐ Blowjob
- ☐ Eating Out
- ☐ Missionary
- ☐ Doggystyle
- ☐ On top
- ☐ Other _____ Write In Your Own

- ☐ Car
- ☐ Bed
- ☐ Kitchen
- ☐ Hotel
- ☐ Outside
- ☐ Other _____ Write In Your Own

- ☐ Quickie
- ☐ 1 Hour
- ☐ Tantric
- ☐ BDSM Play
- ☐ Toys
- ☐ All Night Long

WHEN: ☐ Monday ☐ Tuesday ☐ Wednesday ☐ Thursday ☐ Friday ☐ Saturday ☐ Sunday

To Be Paid By _____ Signed

Back Side Of Check

Tear Here Across This Line

Sex Check 023

DATE: _____

PAY TO THE
ORDER OF: _____

GOING OUT: One Night Of Fun Followed By Sensual Passionate Love

- ☐ Dancing
- ☐ Drinking
- ☐ Movies
- ☐ Bowling
- ☐ Concert
- ☐ Other _____ *Write In Your Own*

- ☐ Blowjob
- ☐ Eating Out
- ☐ Missionary
- ☐ Doggystyle
- ☐ On top
- ☐ Other _____ *Write In Your Own*

- ☐ Car
- ☐ Bed
- ☐ Kitchen
- ☐ Hotel
- ☐ Outside
- ☐ Other _____ *Write In Your Own*

- ☐ Quickie
- ☐ 1 Hour
- ☐ Tantric
- ☐ BDSM Play
- ☐ Toys
- ☐ All Night Long

WHEN: ☐ Monday ☐ Tuesday ☐ Wednesday ☐ Thursday ☐ Friday ☐ Saturday ☐ Sunday

To Be Paid By _____   Signed _____

Back Side Of Check

Tear Here Across This Line

DATE: _____

SEX CHECK 024

PAY TO THE
ORDER OF: _____

GOING OUT: One Night Of Fun Followed By Sensual Passionate Love

- ☐ Dancing
- ☐ Drinking
- ☐ Movies
- ☐ Bowling
- ☐ Concert
- ☐ Other _____ Write In Your Own

- ☐ Blowjob
- ☐ Eating Out
- ☐ Missionary
- ☐ Doggystyle
- ☐ On top
- ☐ Other _____ Write In Your Own

- ☐ Car
- ☐ Bed
- ☐ Kitchen
- ☐ Hotel
- ☐ Outside
- ☐ Other _____ Write In Your Own

- ☐ Quickie
- ☐ 1 Hour
- ☐ Tantric
- ☐ BDSM Play
- ☐ Toys
- ☐ All Night Long

WHEN: ☐ Monday ☐ Tuesday ☐ Wednesday ☐ Thursday ☐ Friday ☐ Saturday ☐ Sunday

To Be Paid By _____   Signed _____

Back Side Of Check

Tear Here Across This Line

SEX CHECK 025

DATE: _____

PAY TO THE
ORDER OF: _____

GOING OUT: One Night Of Fun Followed By Sensual Passionate Love

- ☐ Dancing
- ☐ Drinking
- ☐ Movies
- ☐ Bowling
- ☐ Concert
- ☐ Other _____ *Write In Your Own*

- ☐ Blowjob
- ☐ Eating Out
- ☐ Missionary
- ☐ Doggystyle
- ☐ On top
- ☐ Other _____ *Write In Your Own*

- ☐ Car
- ☐ Bed
- ☐ Kitchen
- ☐ Hotel
- ☐ Outside
- ☐ Other _____ *Write In Your Own*

- ☐ Quickie
- ☐ 1 Hour
- ☐ Tantric
- ☐ BDSM Play
- ☐ Toys
- ☐ All Night Long

WHEN: ☐ Monday ☐ Tuesday ☐ Wednesday ☐ Thursday ☐ Friday ☐ Saturday ☐ Sunday

To Be Paid By _____   Signed _____

Back Side Of Check

Tear Here Across This Line

DATE: _____

Sex Check 02/b

PAY TO THE
ORDER OF: _____

GOING OUT: One Night Of Fun Followed By Sensual Passionate Love

- ☐ Dancing
- ☐ Drinking
- ☐ Movies
- ☐ Bowling
- ☐ Concert
- ☐ Other _____ *Write In Your Own*

- ☐ Blowjob
- ☐ Eating Out
- ☐ Missionary
- ☐ Doggystyle
- ☐ On top
- ☐ Other _____ *Write In Your Own*

- ☐ Car
- ☐ Bed
- ☐ Kitchen
- ☐ Hotel
- ☐ Outside
- ☐ Other _____ *Write In Your Own*

- ☐ Quickie
- ☐ 1 Hour
- ☐ Tantric
- ☐ BDSM Play
- ☐ Toys
- ☐ All Night Long

WHEN: ☐ Monday ☐ Tuesday ☐ Wednesday ☐ Thursday ☐ Friday ☐ Saturday ☐ Sunday

To Be Paid By _____ Signed _____

Back Side Of Check

Tear Here Across This Line

DATE: _____

PAY TO THE
ORDER OF: _____

SEX CHECK 027

GOING OUT: One Night Of Fun Followed By Sensual Passionate Love

- ☐ Dancing
- ☐ Drinking
- ☐ Movies
- ☐ Bowling
- ☐ Concert
- ☐ Other _____ Write In Your Own

- ☐ Blowjob
- ☐ Eating Out
- ☐ Missionary
- ☐ Doggystyle
- ☐ On top
- ☐ Other _____ Write In Your Own

- ☐ Car
- ☐ Bed
- ☐ Kitchen
- ☐ Hotel
- ☐ Outside
- ☐ Other _____ Write In Your Own

- ☐ Quickie
- ☐ 1 Hour
- ☐ Tantric
- ☐ BDSM Play
- ☐ Toys
- ☐ All Night Long

WHEN: ☐ Monday ☐ Tuesday ☐ Wednesday ☐ Thursday ☐ Friday ☐ Saturday ☐ Sunday

To Be Paid By _____   Signed _____

Back Side Of Check

Tear Here Across This Line

DATE: _____

SEX CHECK 028

PAY TO THE
ORDER OF: _____

GOING OUT: One Night Of Fun Followed By Sensual Passionate Love

- ☐ Dancing
- ☐ Drinking
- ☐ Movies
- ☐ Bowling
- ☐ Concert
- ☐ Other _____ Write In Your Own

- ☐ Blowjob
- ☐ Eating Out
- ☐ Missionary
- ☐ Doggystyle
- ☐ On top
- ☐ Other _____ Write In Your Own

- ☐ Car
- ☐ Bed
- ☐ Kitchen
- ☐ Hotel
- ☐ Outside
- ☐ Other _____ Write In Your Own

- ☐ Quickie
- ☐ 1 Hour
- ☐ Tantric
- ☐ BDSM Play
- ☐ Toys
- ☐ All Night Long

WHEN: ☐ Monday ☐ Tuesday ☐ Wednesday ☐ Thursday ☐ Friday ☐ Saturday ☐ Sunday

To Be Paid By _____   Signed _____

Back Side Of Check

Tear Here Across This Line

DATE: _____

SEX CHECK 029

PAY TO THE
ORDER OF: _____

GOING OUT: One Night Of Fun Followed By Sensual Passionate Love

- ☐ Dancing
- ☐ Drinking
- ☐ Movies
- ☐ Bowling
- ☐ Concert
- ☐ Other _____ Write In Your Own

- ☐ Blowjob
- ☐ Eating Out
- ☐ Missionary
- ☐ Doggystyle
- ☐ On top
- ☐ Other _____ Write In Your Own

- ☐ Car
- ☐ Bed
- ☐ Kitchen
- ☐ Hotel
- ☐ Outside
- ☐ Other _____ Write In Your Own

- ☐ Quickie
- ☐ 1 Hour
- ☐ Tantric
- ☐ BDSM Play
- ☐ Toys
- ☐ All Night Long

WHEN: ☐ Monday ☐ Tuesday ☐ Wednesday ☐ Thursday ☐ Friday ☐ Saturday ☐ Sunday

To Be Paid By _____   Signed _____

Back Side Of Check

Tear Here Across This Line

DATE: _____

SEX CHECK 030

PAY TO THE
ORDER OF: _____

GOING OUT: One Night Of Fun Followed By Sensual Passionate Love

- [ ] Dancing
- [ ] Drinking
- [ ] Movies
- [ ] Bowling
- [ ] Concert
- [ ] Other _____ Write In Your Own

- [ ] Blowjob
- [ ] Eating Out
- [ ] Missionary
- [ ] Doggystyle
- [ ] On top
- [ ] Other _____ Write In Your Own

- [ ] Car
- [ ] Bed
- [ ] Kitchen
- [ ] Hotel
- [ ] Outside
- [ ] Other _____ Write In Your Own

- [ ] Quickie
- [ ] 1 Hour
- [ ] Tantric
- [ ] BDSM Play
- [ ] Toys
- [ ] All Night Long

WHEN: ☐ Monday ☐ Tuesday ☐ Wednesday ☐ Thursday ☐ Friday ☐ Saturday ☐ Sunday

To Be Paid By _____ Signed _____

Back Side Of Check

Tear Here Across This Line

DATE: _____

SEX CHECK 031

PAY TO THE
ORDER OF: _____

GOING OUT: One Night Of Fun Followed By Sensual Passionate Love

- ☐ Dancing
- ☐ Drinking
- ☐ Movies
- ☐ Bowling
- ☐ Concert
- ☐ Other _____ Write In Your Own

- ☐ Blowjob
- ☐ Eating Out
- ☐ Missionary
- ☐ Doggystyle
- ☐ On top
- ☐ Other _____ Write In Your Own

- ☐ Car
- ☐ Bed
- ☐ Kitchen
- ☐ Hotel
- ☐ Outside
- ☐ Other _____ Write In Your Own

- ☐ Quickie
- ☐ 1 Hour
- ☐ Tantric
- ☐ BDSM Play
- ☐ Toys
- ☐ All Night Long

WHEN: ☐ Monday ☐ Tuesday ☐ Wednesday ☐ Thursday ☐ Friday ☐ Saturday ☐ Sunday

To Be Paid By _____ Signed _____

Back Side Of Check

Tear Here Across This Line

DATE: _____

Sex Check 032

PAY TO THE
ORDER OF: _____

GOING OUT: One Night Of Fun Followed By Sensual Passionate Love

- ☐ Dancing
- ☐ Drinking
- ☐ Movies
- ☐ Bowling
- ☐ Concert
- ☐ Other _____ Write In Your Own

- ☐ Blowjob
- ☐ Eating Out
- ☐ Missionary
- ☐ Doggystyle
- ☐ On top
- ☐ Other _____ Write In Your Own

- ☐ Car
- ☐ Bed
- ☐ Kitchen
- ☐ Hotel
- ☐ Outside
- ☐ Other _____ Write In Your Own

- ☐ Quickie
- ☐ 1 Hour
- ☐ Tantric
- ☐ BDSM Play
- ☐ Toys
- ☐ All Night Long

WHEN: ☐ Monday ☐ Tuesday ☐ Wednesday ☐ Thursday ☐ Friday ☐ Saturday ☐ Sunday

To Be Paid By _____   Signed _____

Back Side Of Check

Tear Here Across This Line

DATE: _____

SEX CHECK 033

PAY TO THE
ORDER OF: _____

GOING OUT: One Night Of Fun Followed By Sensual Passionate Love

- [ ] Dancing
- [ ] Drinking
- [ ] Movies
- [ ] Bowling
- [ ] Concert
- [ ] Other _____ *Write In Your Own*

- [ ] Blowjob
- [ ] Eating Out
- [ ] Missionary
- [ ] Doggystyle
- [ ] On top
- [ ] Other _____ *Write In Your Own*

- [ ] Car
- [ ] Bed
- [ ] Kitchen
- [ ] Hotel
- [ ] Outside
- [ ] Other _____ *Write In Your Own*

- [ ] Quickie
- [ ] 1 Hour
- [ ] Tantric
- [ ] BDSM Play
- [ ] Toys
- [ ] All Night Long

WHEN:
- [ ] Monday
- [ ] Tuesday
- [ ] Wednesday
- [ ] Thursday
- [ ] Friday
- [ ] Saturday
- [ ] Sunday

To Be Paid By _____ Signed _____

Back Side Of Check

Tear Here Across This Line

DATE: _____

Sex Check 034

PAY TO THE
ORDER OF: _____

GOING OUT: One Night Of Fun Followed By Sensual Passionate Love

- ☐ Dancing
- ☐ Drinking
- ☐ Movies
- ☐ Bowling
- ☐ Concert
- ☐ Other _____ Write In Your Own

- ☐ Blowjob
- ☐ Eating Out
- ☐ Missionary
- ☐ Doggystyle
- ☐ On top
- ☐ Other _____ Write In Your Own

- ☐ Car
- ☐ Bed
- ☐ Kitchen
- ☐ Hotel
- ☐ Outside
- ☐ Other _____ Write In Your Own

- ☐ Quickie
- ☐ 1 Hour
- ☐ Tantric
- ☐ BDSM Play
- ☐ Toys
- ☐ All Night Long

WHEN: ☐ Monday ☐ Tuesday ☐ Wednesday ☐ Thursday ☐ Friday ☐ Saturday ☐ Sunday

To Be Paid By _____   Signed _____

Back Side Of Check

Tear Here Across This Line

DATE: _____

SEX CHECK 035

PAY TO THE
ORDER OF: _____

GOING OUT: One Night Of Fun Followed By Sensual Passionate Love

- ☐ Dancing
- ☐ Drinking
- ☐ Movies
- ☐ Bowling
- ☐ Concert
- ☐ Other _____ Write In Your Own

- ☐ Blowjob
- ☐ Eating Out
- ☐ Missionary
- ☐ Doggystyle
- ☐ On top
- ☐ Other _____ Write In Your Own

- ☐ Car
- ☐ Bed
- ☐ Kitchen
- ☐ Hotel
- ☐ Outside
- ☐ Other _____ Write In Your Own

- ☐ Quickie
- ☐ 1 Hour
- ☐ Tantric
- ☐ BDSM Play
- ☐ Toys
- ☐ All Night Long

WHEN: ☐ Monday ☐ Tuesday ☐ Wednesday ☐ Thursday ☐ Friday ☐ Saturday ☐ Sunday

To Be Paid By _____ Signed _____

Back Side Of Check

Tear Here Across This Line

DATE: _____

SEX CHECK D3/6

PAY TO THE
ORDER OF: _____

GOING OUT: One Night Of Fun Followed By Sensual Passionate Love

- ☐ Dancing
- ☐ Drinking
- ☐ Movies
- ☐ Bowling
- ☐ Concert
- ☐ Other _____ Write In Your Own

- ☐ Blowjob
- ☐ Eating Out
- ☐ Missionary
- ☐ Doggystyle
- ☐ On top
- ☐ Other _____ Write In Your Own

- ☐ Car
- ☐ Bed
- ☐ Kitchen
- ☐ Hotel
- ☐ Outside
- ☐ Other _____ Write In Your Own

- ☐ Quickie
- ☐ 1 Hour
- ☐ Tantric
- ☐ BDSM Play
- ☐ Toys
- ☐ All Night Long

WHEN: ☐ Monday ☐ Tuesday ☐ Wednesday ☐ Thursday ☐ Friday ☐ Saturday ☐ Sunday

To Be Paid By _____   Signed _____

Back Side Of Check

Tear Here Across This Line

DATE: _____

SEX CHECK 037

PAY TO THE
ORDER OF: _____

GOING OUT: One Night Of Fun Followed By Sensual Passionate Love

- ☐ Dancing
- ☐ Drinking
- ☐ Movies
- ☐ Bowling
- ☐ Concert
- ☐ Other _____ *Write In Your Own*

- ☐ Blowjob
- ☐ Eating Out
- ☐ Missionary
- ☐ Doggystyle
- ☐ On top
- ☐ Other _____ *Write In Your Own*

- ☐ Car
- ☐ Bed
- ☐ Kitchen
- ☐ Hotel
- ☐ Outside
- ☐ Other _____ *Write In Your Own*

- ☐ Quickie
- ☐ 1 Hour
- ☐ Tantric
- ☐ BDSM Play
- ☐ Toys
- ☐ All Night Long

WHEN: ☐ Monday ☐ Tuesday ☐ Wednesday ☐ Thursday ☐ Friday ☐ Saturday ☐ Sunday

To Be Paid By _____ Signed _____

Back Side Of Check

Tear Here Across This Line

DATE: _____

SEX CHECK 038

PAY TO THE
ORDER OF: _____

GOING OUT: One Night Of Fun Followed By Sensual Passionate Love

- ☐ Dancing
- ☐ Drinking
- ☐ Movies
- ☐ Bowling
- ☐ Concert
- ☐ Other _____ Write In Your Own

- ☐ Blowjob
- ☐ Eating Out
- ☐ Missionary
- ☐ Doggystyle
- ☐ On top
- ☐ Other _____ Write In Your Own

- ☐ Car
- ☐ Bed
- ☐ Kitchen
- ☐ Hotel
- ☐ Outside
- ☐ Other _____ Write In Your Own

- ☐ Quickie
- ☐ 1 Hour
- ☐ Tantric
- ☐ BDSM Play
- ☐ Toys
- ☐ All Night Long

WHEN: ☐ Monday ☐ Tuesday ☐ Wednesday ☐ Thursday ☐ Friday ☐ Saturday ☐ Sunday

To Be Paid By _____

Signed _____

Back Side Of Check

Tear Here Across This Line

DATE: _____

SEX CHECK 039

PAY TO THE
ORDER OF: _____

GOING OUT: One Night Of Fun Followed By Sensual Passionate Love

- ☐ Dancing
- ☐ Drinking
- ☐ Movies
- ☐ Bowling
- ☐ Concert
- ☐ Other _____ Write In Your Own

- ☐ Blowjob
- ☐ Eating Out
- ☐ Missionary
- ☐ Doggystyle
- ☐ On top
- ☐ Other _____ Write In Your Own

- ☐ Car
- ☐ Bed
- ☐ Kitchen
- ☐ Hotel
- ☐ Outside
- ☐ Other _____ Write In Your Own

- ☐ Quickie
- ☐ 1 Hour
- ☐ Tantric
- ☐ BDSM Play
- ☐ Toys
- ☐ All Night Long

WHEN: ☐ Monday ☐ Tuesday ☐ Wednesday ☐ Thursday ☐ Friday ☐ Saturday ☐ Sunday

To Be Paid By _____   Signed _____

Back Side Of Check

Tear Here Across This Line

DATE: _____

SEX CHECK 04D

PAY TO THE
ORDER OF: _____

GOING OUT: One Night Of Fun Followed By Sensual Passionate Love

- ☐ Dancing
- ☐ Drinking
- ☐ Movies
- ☐ Bowling
- ☐ Concert
- ☐ Other _____ Write In Your Own

- ☐ Blowjob
- ☐ Eating Out
- ☐ Missionary
- ☐ Doggystyle
- ☐ On top
- ☐ Other _____ Write In Your Own

- ☐ Car
- ☐ Bed
- ☐ Kitchen
- ☐ Hotel
- ☐ Outside
- ☐ Other _____ Write In Your Own

- ☐ Quickie
- ☐ 1 Hour
- ☐ Tantric
- ☐ BDSM Play
- ☐ Toys
- ☐ All Night Long

WHEN: ☐ Monday ☐ Tuesday ☐ Wednesday ☐ Thursday ☐ Friday ☐ Saturday ☐ Sunday

To Be Paid By _____   Signed _____

Back Side Of Check

Tear Here Across This Line

DATE: _____

SEX CHECK D411

PAY TO THE
ORDER OF: _____

GOING OUT: One Night Of Fun Followed By Sensual Passionate Love

- ☐ Dancing
- ☐ Drinking
- ☐ Movies
- ☐ Bowling
- ☐ Concert
- ☐ Other _____ *Write In Your Own*

- ☐ Blowjob
- ☐ Eating Out
- ☐ Missionary
- ☐ Doggystyle
- ☐ On top
- ☐ Other _____ *Write In Your Own*

- ☐ Car
- ☐ Bed
- ☐ Kitchen
- ☐ Hotel
- ☐ Outside
- ☐ Other _____ *Write In Your Own*

- ☐ Quickie
- ☐ 1 Hour
- ☐ Tantric
- ☐ BDSM Play
- ☐ Toys
- ☐ All Night Long

WHEN: ☐ Monday ☐ Tuesday ☐ Wednesday ☐ Thursday ☐ Friday ☐ Saturday ☐ Sunday

To Be Paid By _____   Signed _____

Back Side Of Check

Tear Here Across This Line

DATE: _____

SEX CHECK 042

PAY TO THE
ORDER OF: _____

GOING OUT: One Night Of Fun Followed By Sensual Passionate Love

- ☐ Dancing
- ☐ Drinking
- ☐ Movies
- ☐ Bowling
- ☐ Concert
- ☐ Other _____ *Write In Your Own*

- ☐ Blowjob
- ☐ Eating Out
- ☐ Missionary
- ☐ Doggystyle
- ☐ On top
- ☐ Other _____ *Write In Your Own*

- ☐ Car
- ☐ Bed
- ☐ Kitchen
- ☐ Hotel
- ☐ Outside
- ☐ Other _____ *Write In Your Own*

- ☐ Quickie
- ☐ 1 Hour
- ☐ Tantric
- ☐ BDSM Play
- ☐ Toys
- ☐ All Night Long

WHEN: ☐ Monday ☐ Tuesday ☐ Wednesday ☐ Thursday ☐ Friday ☐ Saturday ☐ Sunday

To Be Paid By _____ Signed _____

Back Side Of Check

Tear Here Across This Line

DATE: _____

SEX CHECK 043

PAY TO THE
ORDER OF: _____

GOING OUT: One Night Of Fun Followed By Sensual Passionate Love

- ☐ Dancing
- ☐ Drinking
- ☐ Movies
- ☐ Bowling
- ☐ Concert
- ☐ Other _____ *Write In Your Own*

- ☐ Blowjob
- ☐ Eating Out
- ☐ Missionary
- ☐ Doggystyle
- ☐ On top
- ☐ Other _____ *Write In Your Own*

- ☐ Car
- ☐ Bed
- ☐ Kitchen
- ☐ Hotel
- ☐ Outside
- ☐ Other _____ *Write In Your Own*

- ☐ Quickie
- ☐ 1 Hour
- ☐ Tantric
- ☐ BDSM Play
- ☐ Toys
- ☐ All Night Long

WHEN: ☐ Monday ☐ Tuesday ☐ Wednesday ☐ Thursday ☐ Friday ☐ Saturday ☐ Sunday

To Be Paid By _____   Signed _____

Back Side Of Check

Tear Here Across This Line

DATE: _____

Sex Check 044

PAY TO THE
ORDER OF: _____

GOING OUT: One Night Of Fun Followed By Sensual Passionate Love

- ☐ Dancing
- ☐ Drinking
- ☐ Movies
- ☐ Bowling
- ☐ Concert
- ☐ Other _____ Write In Your Own

- ☐ Blowjob
- ☐ Eating Out
- ☐ Missionary
- ☐ Doggystyle
- ☐ On top
- ☐ Other _____ Write In Your Own

- ☐ Car
- ☐ Bed
- ☐ Kitchen
- ☐ Hotel
- ☐ Outside
- ☐ Other _____ Write In Your Own

- ☐ Quickie
- ☐ 1 Hour
- ☐ Tantric
- ☐ BDSM Play
- ☐ Toys
- ☐ All Night Long

WHEN: ☐ Monday ☐ Tuesday ☐ Wednesday ☐ Thursday ☐ Friday ☐ Saturday ☐ Sunday

To Be Paid By _____   Signed _____

Back Side Of Check

Tear Here Across This Line

DATE: _____

SEX CHECK D4S

PAY TO THE
ORDER OF: _____

GOING OUT: One Night Of Fun Followed By Sensual Passionate Love

- ☐ Dancing
- ☐ Drinking
- ☐ Movies
- ☐ Bowling
- ☐ Concert
- ☐ Other _____ *Write In Your Own*

- ☐ Blowjob
- ☐ Eating Out
- ☐ Missionary
- ☐ Doggystyle
- ☐ On top
- ☐ Other _____ *Write In Your Own*

- ☐ Car
- ☐ Bed
- ☐ Kitchen
- ☐ Hotel
- ☐ Outside
- ☐ Other _____ *Write In Your Own*

- ☐ Quickie
- ☐ 1 Hour
- ☐ Tantric
- ☐ BDSM Play
- ☐ Toys
- ☐ All Night Long

WHEN: ☐ Monday ☐ Tuesday ☐ Wednesday ☐ Thursday ☐ Friday ☐ Saturday ☐ Sunday

To Be Paid By _____   Signed _____

Back Side Of Check

Tear Here Across This Line

DATE: _____

SEX CHECK 04/b

PAY TO THE
ORDER OF: _____

GOING OUT: One Night Of Fun Followed By Sensual Passionate Love

- ☐ Dancing
- ☐ Drinking
- ☐ Movies
- ☐ Bowling
- ☐ Concert
- ☐ Other _____ Write In Your Own

- ☐ Blowjob
- ☐ Eating Out
- ☐ Missionary
- ☐ Doggystyle
- ☐ On top
- ☐ Other _____ Write In Your Own

- ☐ Car
- ☐ Bed
- ☐ Kitchen
- ☐ Hotel
- ☐ Outside
- ☐ Other _____ Write In Your Own

- ☐ Quickie
- ☐ 1 Hour
- ☐ Tantric
- ☐ BDSM Play
- ☐ Toys
- ☐ All Night Long

WHEN: ☐ Monday ☐ Tuesday ☐ Wednesday ☐ Thursday ☐ Friday ☐ Saturday ☐ Sunday

To Be Paid By _____   Signed _____

Back Side Of Check

Tear Here Across This Line

DATE: _____

SEX CHECK 047

PAY TO THE
ORDER OF: _____

GOING OUT: One Night Of Fun Followed By Sensual Passionate Love

- ☐ Dancing
- ☐ Drinking
- ☐ Movies
- ☐ Bowling
- ☐ Concert
- ☐ Other _____ *Write In Your Own*

- ☐ Blowjob
- ☐ Eating Out
- ☐ Missionary
- ☐ Doggystyle
- ☐ On top
- ☐ Other _____ *Write In Your Own*

- ☐ Car
- ☐ Bed
- ☐ Kitchen
- ☐ Hotel
- ☐ Outside
- ☐ Other _____ *Write In Your Own*

- ☐ Quickie
- ☐ 1 Hour
- ☐ Tantric
- ☐ BDSM Play
- ☐ Toys
- ☐ All Night Long

WHEN: ☐ Monday ☐ Tuesday ☐ Wednesday ☐ Thursday ☐ Friday ☐ Saturday ☐ Sunday

To Be Paid By _____ Signed _____

Back Side Of Check

Tear Here Across This Line

DATE: _____

Sex Check 04B

PAY TO THE
ORDER OF: _____

GOING OUT: One Night Of Fun Followed By Sensual Passionate Love

- ☐ Dancing
- ☐ Drinking
- ☐ Movies
- ☐ Bowling
- ☐ Concert
- ☐ Other _____ *Write In Your Own*

- ☐ Blowjob
- ☐ Eating Out
- ☐ Missionary
- ☐ Doggystyle
- ☐ On top
- ☐ Other _____ *Write In Your Own*

- ☐ Car
- ☐ Bed
- ☐ Kitchen
- ☐ Hotel
- ☐ Outside
- ☐ Other _____ *Write In Your Own*

- ☐ Quickie
- ☐ 1 Hour
- ☐ Tantric
- ☐ BDSM Play
- ☐ Toys
- ☐ All Night Long

WHEN: ☐ Monday ☐ Tuesday ☐ Wednesday ☐ Thursday ☐ Friday ☐ Saturday ☐ Sunday

To Be Paid By _____   Signed _____

Back Side Of Check

Tear Here Across This Line

DATE: _____

SEX CHECK 049

PAY TO THE
ORDER OF: _____

GOING OUT: One Night Of Fun Followed By Sensual Passionate Love

- ☐ Dancing
- ☐ Drinking
- ☐ Movies
- ☐ Bowling
- ☐ Concert
- ☐ Other _____ Write In Your Own

- ☐ Blowjob
- ☐ Eating Out
- ☐ Missionary
- ☐ Doggystyle
- ☐ On top
- ☐ Other _____ Write In Your Own

- ☐ Car
- ☐ Bed
- ☐ Kitchen
- ☐ Hotel
- ☐ Outside
- ☐ Other _____ Write In Your Own

- ☐ Quickie
- ☐ 1 Hour
- ☐ Tantric
- ☐ BDSM Play
- ☐ Toys
- ☐ All Night Long

WHEN! ☐ Monday ☐ Tuesday ☐ Wednesday ☐ Thursday ☐ Friday ☐ Saturday ☐ Sunday

To Be Paid By _____ Signed _____

Back Side Of Check

Tear Here Across This Line

DATE: _____

Sex Check 050

PAY TO THE
ORDER OF:

GOING OUT: One Night Of Fun Followed By Sensual Passionate Love

- ☐ Dancing
- ☐ Drinking
- ☐ Movies
- ☐ Bowling
- ☐ Concert
- ☐ Other _____ *Write In Your Own*

- ☐ Blowjob
- ☐ Eating Out
- ☐ Missionary
- ☐ Doggystyle
- ☐ On top
- ☐ Other _____ *Write In Your Own*

- ☐ Car
- ☐ Bed
- ☐ Kitchen
- ☐ Hotel
- ☐ Outside
- ☐ Other _____ *Write In Your Own*

- ☐ Quickie
- ☐ 1 Hour
- ☐ Tantric
- ☐ BDSM Play
- ☐ Toys
- ☐ All Night Long

WHEN: ☐ Monday ☐ Tuesday ☐ Wednesday ☐ Thursday ☐ Friday ☐ Saturday ☐ Sunday

To Be Paid By _____

Signed _____

Back Side Of Check

Other Coupon Books

- 30 Days of Oral Pleasure For Her
- 30 Days of Blowjobs for Him
- New Years Eve Sex Coupons
- And Many More.

Made in the USA
Lexington, KY
04 February 2016